BREAKFAST
for Dinner

BREAKFAST
for Dinner

Morning meals get a makeover in this
sensational collection of rule-breaking recipes

**with recipes
by Carol Hilker**

with photography by
Toby Scott

RYLAND PETERS & SMALL
LONDON • NEW YORK

This book is dedicated to those who sleep-in, those who drink coffee at night and those who like eggs past noon. You know who you are!

Senior Designer Iona Hoyle

Editors Nathan Joyce, Kate Reeves-Brown and Julia Charles

Production Controller Mai-Ling Collyer

Art Director Leslie Harrington

Editorial Director Julia Charles

Publisher Cindy Richards

Food stylist Lizzie Harris

Prop stylist Luis Peral

Indexer Hilary Bird

First published in 2016
by Ryland Peters & Small
20–21 Jockey's Fields
London WC1R 4BW
and
341 East 116th Street
New York NY 10029
www.rylandpeters.com

10 9 8 7 6 5 4 3 2 1

Text © Carol Hilker 2016 (with the exception of recipes listed on page 160) and Ryland Peters & Small 2016
Design and photography © Ryland Peters & Small 2016

ISBN 978-1-84975-703-4

Printed and bound in China

A CIP record for this book is available from the British Library. CIP data from the Library of Congress has been applied for.

Notes

• All spoon measurements are level unless otherwise specified.

• Eggs used in baking recipes in this book are (UK) medium and (US) large unless otherwise stated.

Contents

INTRODUCTION

Cooking breakfast for dinner is one of those things that almost seems a little taboo — much like drinking on a Sunday or skinny dipping. It goes against that run of the mill rules are rules mindset. It's rebellious, it's fun and most importantly, it's for those who have no problem with indulging in the out of the ordinary. Frankly, it's the antidote to what is and what isn't acceptable for traditional home cooks and food lovers. And, in reality, it's a way to declare that your kitchen lives by your own rules and you don't care what anyone else thinks!

If you are someone who comes home after a long day's work and craves something as simple as a plate of scrambled eggs, you've bought the right book! After a day spent working hard and dealing with life in general, sometimes we all just need a comforting meal that will help us reset and for many, that meal is a breakfast dish, be it noon or 2 am. Part of being a responsible adult is learning to support yourself by engaging in some sort of normality (at least sometimes!) — pay your taxes, pay your mortgage, put food in your fridge. At one point, we all learn to take care of ourselves. Part of taking care of yourself is doing things that make you happy. And if something as easy as eating a stack of fluffy pancakes at 10 pm makes you smile, then by all means get to those pancakes!

Although it's a well-known fact that breakfast is the most important meal of the day, most of us are lucky if we get to even get a muffin or a bowl of oatmeal down before rushing out the door to work. Plus many of us wake up and don't immediately feel like filling our bellies with rich, decadent food. This book is all about how to take the best of traditional breakfast foods and turn them into a meal to be savoured any time of day. That being said, if you are going to time travel the breakfast dish and serve it past its bedtime it will need some modifications. A little gussying up if you will... This is a book about breakfast for dinner or 'brinner' as it's affectionately called. Flavoursome and hearty egg dishes, hot sandwiches, waffles, skillets and bowls that pass with flying colours at dinnertime; pastries, coffee cakes and hot beverages that can be enjoyed throughout the day; and cocktails and punches that are equally as intriguing imbibed with brunch as at cocktail 'o' clock.

The food in this book can be eaten any time of day, every day, not just on lazy Sunday mornings. *Enjoy!*

Eggs

the way you like them

EGG IN A HOLE ("BETTY GRABLE EGGS")
with rocket & bacon salad

150 g/1 cup streaky/fatty bacon

80 g/4 cups baby rocket/young arugula leaves, rinsed and dried

about 16 cherry tomatoes, halved

½ red onion, very thinly sliced

2 tablespoons grapeseed oil or olive oil

1 tablespoon rice vinegar

4 slices sourdough bread

4 eggs

salt and freshly ground black pepper

4-5 cm/1½-2 inch round cookie cutter (or other shape, such as heart)

SERVES 4

THE "EGG IN THE HOLE" IS A WHIMSICAL PLAY ON EGGS WITH TOAST THAT HAS MADE ITS MARK THROUGHOUT POP CULTURE. MADE POPULAR BY BETTY GRABLE IN THE 1941 FILM, "MOON OVER MIAMI", IT'S BEEN USED COUNTLESS TIMES IN MOVIES, TV SHOWS AND MOSTLY (AT LEAST IN MY CASE) BY DADS AND GRANDPARENTS. USE A COOKIE CUTTER OR HAND CARVE A SHAPE IN THE MIDDLE OF A PIECE OF BREAD AND FRY THE EGG AND THE BREAD TOGETHER. IT'S SIMPLE. THE RESULT IS A SLIGHTLY RUNNY EGG WITH A TOASTED PIECE OF BREAD PERFECTLY CAPABLE OF SOAKING UP THE YOLK. SERVE ALONGSIDE A ROCKET/ARUGULA SALAD TOPPED WITH BACON FOR A PERFECT BALANCE.

First, make the salad. Fry the bacon in a frying pan/skillet until crisp. Remove the bacon with a slotted spoon and set aside on paper towels to cool. Reserve the grease in the pan. Once cool, chop the bacon into pieces.

In a large plastic bowl with a lid, combine the rocket/arugula, cherry tomatoes, red onion, oil and vinegar. Season with salt and pepper to taste. Cover and shake to mix. Top with the chopped bacon.

Cut a 4–5-cm/1½–2 inch hole from the centre of the bread with the cookie cutter.

For the eggs, heat the bacon over low heat. Lay the bread down in the hot frying pan/skillet. When the side facing down is lightly toasted, about 2 minutes, flip it over and crack the egg into the hole in the middle of the bread.

Season with salt and pepper. Continue to cook until the egg is cooked and mostly firm. Flip again and cook 1 minute more to ensure doneness on both sides. Serve immediately with the salad.

FISHERMAN'S WHARF BENEDICT
on sourdough

4 slices fresh sourdough bread

450 g/3 cups shredded/ picked over good-quality crab meat, at room temperature

8 eggs

120 g/4 oz. Chevre goats' cheese, sliced into quarters

2 ripe avocados, halved, stoned/pitted and sliced

Lemon hollandaise

6 egg yolks

finely grated zest of 1 small lemon

2 tablespoons Dijon mustard

340 g/1½ cups unsalted butter, melted

½ teaspoon salt

⅛ teaspoon freshly ground black pepper

⅛ teaspoon paprika

a double boiler (optional)

SERVES 4

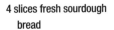

THIS TAKE ON THE CLASSIC EGGS BENEDICT IS A FITTING ODE TO SAN FRANCISCO'S FAMED FISHERMAN'S WHARF; A BEAUTIFUL PART OF THE CITY, WHERE ABOUT A DOZEN SEAFOOD SHACKS EXIST. ONE CAN GRAB A CRAB SANDWICH AND EAT IT AMONGST A BACKDROP OF SEAGULLS AND SEA AIR. THIS BENEDICT IS MY TRIBUTE TO FISHERMAN'S WHARF. IT USES SOURDOUGH BREAD, A LEMON HOLLANDAISE AND CHEVRE CHEESE AND AVOCADO (TWO OTHER THINGS CALIFORNIA DOES WELL!).

Start by making the lemon hollandaise. In a small saucepan or pot set over low heat, bring 5 cm/2 inches of water to a bare simmer. Place a metal bowl over the pot to form a bain-marie.

Add the yolks, lemon zest and mustard to the bowl of the bain-marie and whisk constantly until the mixture is thickened and ribbons form when you pull this whisk away from the bowl (should take about 4–5 minutes). The yolks should double to triple in volume.

Slowly whisk in the melted butter, stirring constantly. Once the butter is fully incorporated, add the salt, pepper and paprika and continue whisking for about 3 minutes, until thick. If the mixture is too thick, add a little hot water as needed. Adjust the seasoning to taste. Remove from the heat and set aside.

Preheat the oven to 230°C (450°F) Gas 8. Cut the sourdough bread in half and arrange on a baking sheet in a single layer. Bake until toasted, about 5 minutes. Put two sourdough halves on each plate and top with crab, dividing evenly.

To poach the eggs, bring 2.5 cm/1 inch water to the boil in a medium pan. Lower the heat so that small bubbles form on the bottom of the pan and break to the surface only occasionally. Crack the eggs into the water one at a time, holding the shells close to the water's surface and letting the eggs slide out gently. Poach the eggs, in two batches to keep them from crowding, 6 minutes for soft-cooked. Lift the eggs out with a slotted spoon, pat dry with a paper towel, and place one egg on each crab-topped sourdough half.

Top each egg with 2–3 tablespoons of the lemon hollandaise (gently reheated if necessary), and top with the goats' cheese and sliced avocado. Serve immediately.

New Orleans BENEDICT

4 eggs

4 un-sugared beignets (see page 129) or un-sugared doughnuts, sliced in half

4 Cajun-style andouille sausages, cooked and sliced (or other spicy smoked pork sausage)

2 spring onions/scallions, thinly sliced

Cajun hollandaise

8 egg yolks

1 tablespoon of finely grated lemon zest

60 ml/¼ cup freshly squeezed lemon juice

285 g/2½ sticks unsalted butter, melted

a little hot water, if needed

½ teaspoon garlic powder

½ teaspoon onion powder

½ teaspoon Kosher salt

¼ teaspoon smoked paprika

¼ teaspoon celery salt

¼ teaspoon dried dill

¼ teaspoon cayenne pepper

SERVES 4

BY USING A PLAIN BEIGNET INSTEAD OF AN ENGLISH MUFFIN, THIS EGGS BENEDICT RECIPE GETS A LITTLE NEW ORLEANS FLAIR. IF THE DOUGHNUT IS TOO MUCH, GO AHEAD AND SUBSTITUTE WITH FRENCH BREAD. EITHER WAY, THE TEXTURES AND TASTES COME TOGETHER PERFECTLY TO BRING A LITTLE OF THE BAYOU TO YOUR KITCHEN.

Start by making the Cajun hollandaise. In a small saucepan or pot set over low heat, bring 5 cm/2 inches of water to a bare simmer. Place a metal bowl over the pot to form a bain-marie.

Add the yolks, half of the lemon juice and all of the zest to the bowl of the bain-marie and whisk constantly until the mixture is thickened and ribbons form when you pull this whisk away (should take about 4–5 minutes). The yolks should double to triple in volume.

Slowly whisk in the melted butter, stirring constantly. If the mixture is too thick, add a little hot water as needed. Once the butter is fully incorporated, stir in the second half of lemon juice and all the spices. Turn off the heat but keep the mixture over the hot water to help maintain the heat.

To poach the eggs, bring 2.5 cm/1 inch water to the boil in a medium pan. Lower the heat so that small bubbles form on the bottom of the pan and break to the surface only occasionally. Crack the eggs into the water one at a time, holding the shells close to the water's surface and letting the eggs slide out gently. Poach the eggs, in two batches to keep them from crowding, 6 minutes for soft-cooked. Lift the eggs out with a slotted spoon and pat dry with a paper towel.

Arrange the halved doughnuts or beignets on plates and carefully place a few slices of the cooked andouille sausage and a poached egg on top of one half. Cover in Cajun hollandaise, finish with sliced spring onion/scallions and top with the other beignet or doughnut half. Serve immediately.

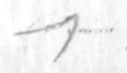

Fried Green Tomato Benedict

2 large green tomatoes, thickly sliced (about 6 slices per tomato)

120 g/¾ cup cornmeal/polenta

8 eggs

12 slices smoked ham, thinly sliced

vegetable oil, for frying (bonus points if you have bacon drippings)

salt and freshly ground black pepper

Spiced hollandaise

80 ml/⅓ cup red wine vinegar

8–10 peppercorns

1 small bay leaf

1 teaspoon ground nutmeg

6 egg yolks

225 g/1 cup unsalted butter, melted

1½ teaspoons of salt, or to taste

½ teaspoon of cayenne pepper

SERVES 4

FRIED GREEN TOMATOES ARE A PERFECT SUMMER DISH. THIS CAN BE SERVED AS A SIDE DISH OR AS THE MAIN STAR WHEN PLATED ALONGSIDE A SIMPLE SALAD. THIS IS A FUN SOUTHERN-STYLE BENEDICT THAT CAN ALSO BE MODIFIED FOR VEGETARIANS.

Start by making the spiced hollandaise. In a small saucepan set over low heat combine the vinegar, peppercorns, bay leaf and nutmeg. Reduce the mixture to 4 tablespoons. Remove from the heat and strain the peppercorns and bay leaf. Set aside to cool.

Place the egg yolks in the bowl of a stand mixer fitted with the whisk attachment, and slowly beat in the reduced vinegar mixture. With the mixer running on medium-high, slowly drizzle in the melted butter until it has all been added. Whisk in the salt and pepper. Set aside.

Sprinkle the tomato slices liberally on both sides with seasoned salt and a few turns of cracked black pepper. Dredge the tomatoes liberally in cornmeal/polenta, and pat them to fully and evenly coat. Set aside the tomatoes while you heat the oil.

Heat about 1 cm/½ inch of oil in a large frying pan/skillet set over medium heat. When the oil is hot, fry the tomatoes until the crust is golden brown and crisp on both sides, about 2–3 minutes per side. Remove and place on a flat baking sheet and blot with paper towels.

To poach the eggs, bring 2.5 cm/1 inch water to the boil in a medium pan. Lower the heat so that small bubbles form on the bottom of the pan and break to the surface only occasionally. Crack the eggs into the water one at a time, holding the shells close to the water's surface and letting the eggs slide out gently. Poach the eggs, in two batches to keep them from crowding, 6 minutes for soft-cooked. Lift the eggs out with a slotted spoon and pat dry with a paper towel.

Place two slices of tomato on a plate, overlapping the slices slightly. Pile on two thin slices of ham, and top the ham with two poached eggs. Spoon a tablespoonful or two of the Hollandaise over the eggs. Repeat with the remaining portions. Serve immediately.

Paris-style EGGS BENEDICT

60 g/¼ cup butter

4 slices bacon

2 teaspoons white or rice vinegar

8 slices Brie cheese

4 eggs

4 pretzel croissants

butter, for spreading

a dash of Tabasco sauce (optional)

a couple of sprigs flat-leaf parsley, chopped, to garnish

freshly ground black pepper

Classic hollandaise

140 g/⅔ cup unsalted butter

3 egg yolks

1 tablespoon freshly squeezed lemon juice

½ teaspoon salt

SERVES 4

THIS VARIANT ON A TRADITIONAL FRENCH BREAKFAST COMES WITH BACON, BRIE AND POACHED EGGS, ALL ASSEMBLED ON TOP OF A PRETZEL CROISSANT AND DRIZZLED WITH HOLLANDAISE SAUCE. THIS DECADENT AND DELICIOUS DISH MAKES THE PERFECT LAZY SUNDAY BRUNCH OR, IF YOU'RE IN THE MOOD, A FUN BREAKFAST-FOR-DINNER. IF YOU CAN'T FIND PRETZEL CROISSANTS, A NORMAL CROISSANT WORKS JUST AS WELL.

To make the hollandaise sauce, melt the butter in a small saucepan. Put the egg yolks, lemon juice and salt in a blender and blend on medium to medium-high speed for 25 seconds or until the eggs lighten in colour. Change the blender speed to the lowest setting and very slowly, pour in the hot butter and continue to blend. Add salt and lemon juice to taste. Transfer to a small jug/pitcher.

Melt some butter in a large frying pan/skillet over low to medium heat, and when the pan is hot, add the bacon, turning it occasionally until warm.

While the bacon is cooking, fill a large saucepan with water and bring to the boil. Add the vinegar and let it come to a boil again. After the water boils, reduce the heat to a simmer.

Next, poach the eggs. The easiest way is to do one egg at a time. Crack the egg into a small bowl and slip it into the barely simmering water. Once the egg begins to solidify, slip in the next egg and so on until you have all 4 cooking. Turn the heat off, cover the pan with a lid and let the eggs sit for 3–4 minutes, depending on how runny you like your eggs. Starting with the first egg you cracked, gently lift them out with a slotted spoon and set them down in a bowl or on a plate.

Toast and butter the croissants. Top with the bacon, 2 slices of Brie and a poached egg. Sprinkle on Tabasco sauce if desired. Pour the hollandaise sauce over the top and garnish with flat-leaf parsley and ground black pepper to taste.

Maine LOBSTER OMELETTE

6 eggs

170 g/6 oz. fresh lobster meat, chopped

10 g/2 teaspoons unsalted butter

sea salt and ground black pepper

115 g/4 oz. tomatoes, chopped

1 teaspoon chives, chopped/snipped

Truffle hollandaise

3 egg yolks

60 ml/¼ cup water

2 tablespoons freshly squeezed lemon juice

115 g/½ cup cold, unsalted butter, cut into pieces

¼ teaspoon sea salt

a pinch of freshly ground black pepper

a pinch of paprika

a drizzle of truffle oil

1 chive, chopped/snipped, to garnish

SERVES 2

ACCORDING TO FOOD LORE, THE OMELETTE/OMELET HAS BEEN AROUND SINCE THE 16TH CENTURY. SINCE THEN, MANY VARIATIONS HAVE EMERGED, FROM THE HAM, GREEN (BELL) PEPPER AND ONION COMBINATION IN A DENVER OMELETTE/OMELET TO KHAGINEH, AN IRANIAN VERSION IN WHICH EGGS ARE BEATEN WITH SUGAR. THE LOBSTER OMELETTE/OMELET IS POPULAR ON THE EAST COAST OF THE US, AND IS ESPECIALLY DECADENT WHEN SERVED WITH TRUFFLE-HOLLANDAISE SAUCE.

Preheat an oven to 110°C (225°F) Gas ¼.

To make the truffle hollandaise, whisk the egg yolks, water and lemon juice in a small saucepan until blended. Cook over very low heat, stirring constantly, until the mixture bubbles at the edges. Stir in the butter, a piece at a time, until it has melted and until the sauce has thickened. Remove from the heat immediately and stir in the salt, pepper, paprika and truffle oil. Transfer the sauce to a small pot, ready to serve.

Whisk the eggs together, then separate the mixture into two bowls and set aside.

Spread the lobster onto an oven-proof dish and place in the preheated oven for 5 minutes.

Over medium heat, warm a medium to large non-stick frying pan/skillet and add half the butter. As the butter melts, season one portion of the eggs with salt and black pepper. Add this egg mixture to the heated frying pan/skillet and stir gently with a spatula.

As the eggs start to set, add half the chopped lobster, half the tomatoes and half the chives to the eggs and stir gently. Stop stirring and allow them to form for 1–2 minutes. Fold the omelette/omelet and slide it out onto a warm plate. Place the plate in the oven to keep the omelette/omelet warm. Repeat the same process for the second omelette/omelet. Serve imediately with the truffle hollandaise on the side.

Huevos Rancheros

½ tablespoon olive oil

8 slices of back or streaky/fatty bacon, finely chopped

1 large onion, finely chopped

1 garlic clove, crushed

4 hot green chillies/chiles, finely chopped

1 mild red chilli/chile, deseeded and finely chopped

4 tomatoes, skinned and roughly chopped

½ teaspoon sea salt

¼ teaspoon freshly ground black pepper

8 eggs

4 plain 20-cm/8-inch flour tortillas

fresh tomato salsa, to serve

Serves 4

This dish is hot! It is often served for brunch with a Bloody Mary as something of a hangover cure. If you prefer it slightly milder, reduce the amount of fiery green chilli/chile appropriately. Top it all off with a salsa. This is best eaten outside in the sunshine at your favourite table wearing very dark sunglasses!

Heat the oil in a frying pan/skillet and gently fry the bacon until almost cooked. Drain off all but 1 teaspoon of the fat.

Add the onion and garlic to the pan and cook, allowing to lightly brown. Add the chillies/chiles, tomatoes, salt and pepper, stir well and cover. Bring to the boil, reduce the heat and simmer for about 20 minutes, stirring frequently.

Meanwhile, fry or poach the eggs to your taste and gently warm the tortillas in a frying pan/skillet or warm oven, or under the grill/broiler.

To serve, place 2 eggs per person on a warmed tortilla and liberally spoon the salsa over the eggs. Eat immediately!

SPANISH TORTILLA
with roasted piquillo peppers

50 ml/3 tablespoons olive oil

2 large white onions, thinly sliced

2 large potatoes, peeled and thinly sliced

4 roasted Piquillo peppers, roughly chopped

6 eggs

sea salt and freshly ground black pepper

green salad, to serve

a large, heavy-based, lidded frying pan/skillet (about 28-cm/11-inch) plus a plate slightly larger than the frying pan/skillet

SERVES 2

HERE ARE SIMPLE INGREDIENTS, CAREFULLY COOKED WITH A LITTLE CHILLI/CHILE TWIST. IT REALLY IS HARD TO GO WRONG WITH A TORTILLA. EATEN HOT OR COLD, FOR LUNCH, SUPPER OR EVEN AS A MAIN MEAL, IT IS ALWAYS WELCOME. IT IS WORTH REMEMBERING THAT THIS IS NOT ANYTHING LIKE A FRENCH OMELETTE/OMELET; IT REQUIRES COMPARABLY LONG AND GENTLE COOKING. LIKE THE ITALIAN FRITTATA IT IS, HOWEVER, ALWAYS WORTH THE WAIT.

Heat half the oil in the large, heavy-based frying pan/skillet, add the onions and potatoes and toss to coat. Season well and add the Piquillo peppers. Turn down the heat and cover with a lid. Cook until the potatoes and onions are soft and translucent, about 20 minutes. Turn regularly to prevent too much browning. Once they are softened, remove them from the oil with a slotted spoon and set aside.

Lightly whisk the eggs in a large mixing bowl and add the onions and potatoes (they should still be hot so that the cooking process of the eggs begins as soon as they are mixed together). Season with salt and pepper. Add the rest of the oil to the pan and return to medium heat. Pour the egg mixture into the hot pan – it should fill it by about two-thirds. Turn the heat down to its lowest setting and cook for 20–25 minutes until there is very little liquid on the surface.

Take the plate that is slightly larger than the frying pan/skillet and place it upside down over the frying pan/skillet. Invert the plate and pan, tipping the tortilla out onto the plate. Put the pan back on the heat and gently slide the tortilla back into it. The cooked side is now facing upward and the uncooked side will now be on the heat. Cook for a further 2–3 minutes. Turn off the heat and let settle. (If you don't feel up to flipping the tortilla over, you can grill/broil the top for 2–3 minutes.)

Turn the tortilla out onto a clean plate and slice to serve. Add a splash of hot sauce, if you like. And it's great with a green salad and a glass of good Spanish Rioja.

Baked Chilli Eggs

25 g/2 tablespoons butter

1 garlic clove, crushed

125 g/4 oz. smoked ham, chopped

225 g/8 oz. mushrooms, diced

2 hot green chillies/chiles, finely chopped

225 ml/scant 1 cup sour cream

2 teaspoons dried parsley

½ teaspoon dried oregano

6 eggs

200 g/2 cups grated/shredded mature/sharp Cheddar cheese

sea salt and freshly ground black pepper

toast, rubbed with a garlic clove, to serve

hot sauce, to serve

6 individual ovenproof ramekins

SERVES 6

THIS IS A WONDERFULLY WARMING AND COMFORTING DISH – A VERSION OF CHILES CON HUEVOS – LONG ASSOCIATED WITH THE LONG, HOT DAYS AND EVEN LONGER, FROSTY NIGHTS OF THE VAST FLAT PLAINS OF THE TEXAS PANHANDLE. THIS DISH ORIGINATED IN THE MEXICAN BORDER COUNTRY BUT IS NOW FAIRLY COMMONLY FOUND THROUGHOUT THE UNITED STATES. ALTHOUGH THIS RECIPE IS OFTEN COOKED IN A SINGLE CASSEROLE DISH, IN THIS VERSION THE MIXTURE IS DIVIDED INTO INDIVIDUAL RAMEKINS BEFORE THE EGGS ARE ADDED, AND SERVED AS A LIGHT MEAL. IT IS IDEAL FOR BREAKFAST OR AS A SUPPER TREAT.

Preheat the oven to 190°C (375°F) Gas 5.

Melt the butter in a heavy-based frying pan/skillet over medium heat and fry the garlic and ham for about 2 minutes, stirring regularly to prevent the garlic from burning. Add the mushrooms and chillies/chiles and continue to cook for about 5–10 minutes until the mushrooms start to brown and the chillies/chiles begin to soften. Remove from the heat and stir in the sour cream, parsley and oregano. Season lightly with salt and pepper. Divide the mixture equally between the ramekins and let stand for about 10 minutes to allow the flavours to blend.

Make a shallow hollow in each mixture and carefully break an egg into each. Season the eggs with salt and pepper. Bake in the preheated oven for about 20–25 minutes or until the egg whites have set. Remove the ramekins from the oven and sprinkle the grated/shredded cheese over all of them. Return to the oven for about 5 minutes, or until the cheese is bubbling. Serve immediately with garlicky toast and a bottle of hot sauce to splash on the eggs.

Tips: If it is very warm in your kitchen, place the mixture in the fridge to set a little before making the hollows and adding the eggs.

For an even more luxurious (and meat-free) alternative, substitute the smoked ham for smoked salmon. Serve with a lightly dressed baby leaf salad.

Hot sandwiches and savoury waffles

Ingredients

- 30 g/2 tablespoons butter
- 4 small ciabatta rolls or brioche buns, split
- 12 thin slices mortadella/bologna
- 2 tablespoons vegetable oil
- 4 eggs
- 4 slices mature/sharp Cheddar cheese
- 2 handfuls rocket/arugula
- ½ ripe tomato, thinly sliced
- ½ red onion, thinly sliced
- green hot sauce, such as Tabasco Green Pepper Sauce, to taste (optional)
- mustard, to serve (optional)
- salt and freshly ground black pepper
- steak fries, to serve (see recipe below), optional

Steak fries

- 4 large baking potatoes, peeled
- 4 tablespoons olive oil
- 2 teaspoons paprika
- 2 teaspoons garlic powder
- 2 teaspoons chilli/chili powder
- 2 teaspoons onion powder

Dill mayo

- 125 ml/½ cup mayonnaise
- a handful fresh chopped dill
- 1 tablespoon freshly squeezed lemon juice
- 1 teaspoon crushed/minced garlic
- salt and white pepper

heavy frying pan/skillet

SERVES 4

FRIED "BALONEY" SANDWICH
with dill mayo & steak fries

ALTHOUGH IT'S SPELLED "BOLOGNA", IT'S REALLY JUST "BALONEY" TO US IN THE STATES. BOLOGNA IS A MEAT THAT ORIGINATED IN BOLOGNA, ITALY. IT'S A MORTADELLA THAT IS FORMED WITH PORK AND LARD, ALTHOUGH IT'S ALSO A FORM OF MEAT THAT CAN BE MADE WITH CHICKEN, TURKEY AND BEEF. IT'S A HOUSEHOLD STAPLE IN MANY REFRIGERATORS AND HAS HELD A PRETTY GOOD STAKE IN LUNCH BOXES FOR A LONG TIME, TOO. THIS VERSION MIXES THE OLD WITH THE NEW – BOLOGNA, CHEESE, LETTUCE, TOMATO, ONION AND MUSTARD. ADD AN EGG AND A DILL MAYO TO GIVE THIS OLD SANDWICH ITS DAY IN THE SUN.

For the steak fries, preheat the oven to 230°C (450°F) Gas 8.

Cut the peeled potatoes into wedges (6–8 per potato depending on their size) and put on a baking sheet.

Put all the other ingredients in a bowl and whisk with a fork to combine. Pour over the potato wedges and use your hands to toss them in the oil until well coated.

Bake in the preheated oven for 45 minutes until cooked through and crisp.

Meanwhile, make up the dill mayo by combining all the ingredients in a small bowl and stirring to mix. Cover with clingfilm/plastic wrap and put in the fridge until ready to serve.

Once the steak fries are nearly cooked, heat a medium heavy frying pan/skillet over medium-high heat.

Spread butter on the cut sides of the rolls/buns and toast in the frying pan/skillet over medium heat until golden brown. Set aside. Add the mortadella/bologna slices to the frying pan/skillet and warm until slightly crisped, 2–3 minutes per side. (You might have to do in two batches.) Set aside.

Add the oil to the frying pan/skillet and crack two eggs, (don't break the yolks!). Fry the eggs over medium-low heat, until the egg white has set but the yolk is still soft, about 3–4 minutes. Season the eggs with salt and pepper. Place the meat on the bottom bun, followed by the egg, cheese, rocket/arugula, tomato, onions, hot sauce and mustard, if using. Spread the bottom of the top buns with 1–2 tablespoons of the dill mayo and close the sandwiches.

Serve immediately with the steak fries and extra dill mayo for dipping.

CHILAQUILE BURGER

900 g/2 lb. minced/
ground beef

750 ml/3 cups Arrabbiata
Sauce (see recipe below)

30 g/2 tablespoons butter

60 g/2 cups thick-cut plain
tortilla chips

4 burger buns, split and
toasted

100 g/1 cup grated/
shredded Cheddar
cheese

170 g/6 oz./1 cup jarred
pickled chilli peppers/
pepperoncini, chopped

Arrabbiata sauce

1 tablespoon vegetable oil

1 large onion, chopped

4 garlic cloves, crushed/
minced

2 x 400-g/14-oz. cans
chopped tomatoes

2 tablespoons tomato
purée/paste

75 ml/⅓ cup white wine

1 tablespoon white sugar

1 teaspoon chilli flakes/
hot red pepper flakes,
crushed

½ teaspoon Italian
seasoning (optional)

1 tablespoon each freshly
chopped basil and
flat-leaf parsley

salt and freshly ground
black pepper

SERVES 4

THIS BURGER IS A TAKE ON THE TRADITIONAL MEXICAN BREAKFAST DISH, CHILAQUILES. A REGULAR BURGER RECIPE GOES FROM AVERAGE TO AMAZING WITH THE ADDITION OF PEPPERONCINI, TORTILLA CHIPS AND SPICY ARRABBIATA SAUCE.

Form the minced/ground beef into four thin 225-g/8-oz burger patties.

Set a griddle/grill pan over medium-high heat. Season the burgers on one side with salt and pepper. When hot, add the burgers to the grill, seasoned-side down. Season the other side of the burger with salt and pepper. Cook to desired doneness.

In a medium frying pan/skillet, heat the arrabbiata sauce over medium heat. Add the butter and stir until it is melted. When the butter is melted add the tortilla chips to the pan. Gently stir the pan to coat the chips while taking care not to break them. Set aside and keep warm.

Place a cooked burger on the bottom half of each burger bun, top with the tortilla mixture (chilaquiles), cheese and the chopped pepperoncini before adding the top of the bun. Serve immediately.

To make the arrabbiata sauce, add the vegetable oil to a large saucepan or pot set over medium heat. When the oil is hot add the chopped onion and garlic. Sauté for 5 minutes, or until softened.

Add the canned tomatoes, tomato paste/purée, wine, sugar, chilli flakes/hot red pepper flakes and Italian seasoning (if using). Season well with salt and black pepper and bring to the boil. Reduce the heat to medium and simmer, uncovered, for about 15 minutes, stirring occasionally. Stir in the basil and parsley, check the seasoning and add more salt and pepper to taste. Use in the recipe above as directed. Any leftover sauce can be frozen for another time.

Fried Chicken & Biscuit Sliders
with Sausage Gravy

4 boneless chicken thighs, skin on

250 ml/1 cup buttermilk

3½ teaspoons chilli flakes/hot red pepper flakes

1¼ tablespoons cayenne pepper

1 tablespoon salt

130 g/1 cup plain/ all-purpose flour

½ tablespoon garlic powder

2 eggs

½ tablespoon apple cider vinegar

40 g/½ cup breadcrumbs

35 g/¼ cup stone-ground yellow grits or polenta

canola oil, for deep-frying

Sage Biscuits and Sausage Gravy (see page opposite), to serve

MAKES 12

THESE SLIDERS USE CHICKEN THIGHS AND ARE THE EPITOME OF A BREAKFAST IN THE SOUTHERN STATES OF THE US AT ITS FINEST. CRUSTED CHICKEN THIGH WITH DILL PICKLES AND HONEY SMEARED ON A SAGE-BISCUIT, ALL SERVED WITH A SAUSAGE GRAVY ON THE SIDE.

The night before you'd like to make these sliders, cut the chicken into 12 bite-sized pieces. Combine in a bag with the buttermilk, chilli flakes/hot red pepper flakes, cayenne pepper and salt. Seal and refrigerate overnight.

The next day, heat 5 cm/2 inches oil in a frying pan/skillet or a deep-fryer to 180°C (350°F). In one bowl, combine half the flour with the garlic powder. In a second bowl, whisk together the eggs and apple cider vinegar. In a third bowl combine the remaining flour, breadcrumbs and grits/polenta.

Once the oil is hot, take the chicken, two or three pieces at a time, from the buttermilk and shake the excess buttermilk off. Dredge in the flour mixture, then in the eggs, and then in the flour and breadcrumbs. Make sure the chicken is completely coated in the third mixture and then drop carefully into the hot oil. Fry for 3–5 minutes, turning as necessary, until golden brown, crisp and cooked through. Transfer onto a rack to cool. Repeat until all of the chicken is fried.

Preheat the oven to 230°C (450°F) Gas 8.

To make the sage biscuits, combine the dry ingredients and sage in a bowl, or in the bowl of a food processor. Add the cubed butter and cut into the flour until it resembles coarse meal. Handle the dough as little as possible. Add the buttermilk and mix just until combined. If it appears on the dry side, add a bit more buttermilk. It should be very wet.

Turn the dough out onto a floured board. Gently, gently pat (do not roll with a rolling pin) the dough out until it's about 1 cm/½ inch thick. Fold the dough about 5 times, then gently press the dough down to 2.5 cm/1 inch thick. Use the cutter to cut the dough into 12 rounds.

Place the biscuits on a baking sheet. If you like soft sides, put them touching each other. If you like crusty sides, put them about 2.5 cm/1 inch apart (these will not rise as high as those put close together). Brush the tops with melted butter and season lightly with salt. Bake in the preheated oven for 10–12 minutes, until light golden brown on top and bottom.

Sage biscuits

260 g/2 cups unbleached plain/all-purpose flour, plus extra for dusting

¼ teaspoon bicarbonate of soda/baking soda

1 tablespoon baking powder

1 teaspoon Kosher salt or regular salt, plus extra for seasoning

a small bunch of sage, thinly sliced

85 g/6 tablespoons unsalted butter, very cold, cubed

250 ml/1 cup buttermilk

60 g/¼ cup butter, melted, for brushing

honey, for drizzling

2 large dill pickles, sliced

7.5-cm/3-inch round plain cookie cutter

MAKES 12

Sausage gravy

450 g/1 lb sage-flavoured pork sausage

1 yellow onion, finely chopped

1–2 tablespoons butter, if needed (see method)

50 g/6 tablespoons plain/all-purpose flour

½ teaspoon poultry seasoning (or crumbled chicken Bouillon or stock cubes)

½ teaspoon ground nutmeg

1–2 dashes of Worcestershire sauce, to taste

1–2 dashes of hot sauce

¼ teaspoon salt

1 litre/4 cups full-fat/whole milk

SERVES 4

Meanwhile, make the sausage gravy. Preheat a 4 litre/4 quart saucepan or pot over medium-high heat. Crumble the sausage into the pan and let it brown for a minute or two, then turn down to medium heat. Continue cooking, breaking up the sausage into smaller pieces, until no pink remains. Stir in the onion and cook until soft and transparent.

Remove the sausage with a slotted spatula or spoon, leaving the fat in the pan. If less than 3 tablespoons of fat remain, add enough butter to make it up to 3 tablespoons. Add the cooked sausage back to the pan on medium heat, and sprinkle the flour over the sausage. Stir in the flour and cook for about 6-8 minutes, until the mixture starts bubbling and turns slightly golden brown.

Stir in the poultry seasoning, nutmeg, Worcestershire sauce, hot sauce and salt. Cook for 1 minute to deepen the flavours. Slowly add the milk and cook over medium heat, stirring occasionally, until thickened, about 15 minutes.

When you are ready to serve, halve the warm scones/biscuits and smear generously with honey. Place a fried chicken bite and a dill pickle slice on each one and serve, with the hot sausage gravy on the side for spooning.

Lemongrass beef

100 g/3½ oz. beef, thinly sliced

1 lemongrass stalk, finely chopped

1 garlic clove, finely chopped

1 shallot, finely chopped

1 teaspoon Maggi Seasoning (or soy sauce)

1 teaspoon pork, chicken or vegetable bouillon

1 teaspoon sugar

Pickle

2 carrots, shredded

½ daikon/mooli, shredded

5 tablespoons cider vinegar

5 tablespoons sugar

To fill

1 Vietnamese baguette or freshly baked, small French baguette

butter or soft cheese

pork or chicken liver pâté

chà chiên Vietnamese ham, thinly sliced

coriander/cilantro

cucumber, cut into 10 cm/4 inch slivers

spring onions/scallions, thinly sliced lengthways

Bird's Eye chillies/chiles, thinly sliced

Maggi Seasoning

Sriracha chilli/chile sauce

SERVES 1–2

LEMONGRASS BEEF BAGUETTE
(Bánh mi)

BÁNH MÌ IS A VIETNAMESE BAGUETTE ORIGINALLY INSPIRED BY THE FRENCH AND NOW A STAPLE IN VIETNAMESE CUISINE. IT HAS A LIGHT, CRUNCHY EXTERIOR AND A DELICATELY FLUFFY INSIDE; SOME DESCRIBE BITING INTO ONE AS BITING INTO CRISPY AIR. AS WITH MOST VIETNAMESE FOOD, THE LIGHTNESS OF THE INGREDIENTS YOU FILL IT WITH IS VITAL – NO ONE RELISHES BEING WEIGHED DOWN. THE DOUGH IN THE CENTRE OF THE BAGUETTE IS REMOVED SO THAT YOU BITE STRAIGHT THROUGH THE LOVELY CRISP CRUST TO THE FILLING WITHIN.

A TYPICAL BÁNH MÌ CONTAINS A FLAVOURSOME COMBINATION OF INGREDIENTS, THE PERFECT EQUILIBRIUM OF SWEET AND SOUR. IF YOU CANNOT BUY AN AUTHENTIC VIETNAMESE BAGUETTE, USE A REGULAR FRENCH BAGUETTE.

Preheat the oven to 220°C (425°F) Gas 7.

Mix all the ingredients for the lemongrass beef in a bowl and marinate for 10 minutes. Transfer to a roasting pan and bake in the preheated oven for 15 minutes.

Mix all the pickle ingredients in a bowl and allow to rest for 15 minutes. Drain and wring with your hands.

To fill, slit the baguette lengthways and pull out the soft doughy inside (which can be used for breadcrumbs). Spread with butter or soft cheese and a smear of pâté. Layer the warm beef and its juices, pickle, chà chiên, coriander/cilantro, cucumber, spring onions/scallions and chillies/chiles over the top and squirt over a few drops of Maggi Seasoning and chilli/chile sauce. Enjoy!

Omelette Baguette

Omelette

2 eggs, beaten

2 spring onions/scallions, thinly sliced

½ teaspoon sugar

a pinch of salt

a pinch of black pepper

1 teaspoon soy sauce

1 tablespoon cooking oil

2 Asian shallots, finely chopped

Pickle

2 carrots, shredded

½ daikon/mooli, shredded

5 tablespoons cider vinegar

5 tablespoons sugar

To fill

2 Vietnamese baguettes or freshly baked, small French baguettes

butter

coriander/cilantro

Bird's Eye chillies/chiles, thinly sliced (deseeded for less heat)

SERVES 1–2

A FRESHLY BAKED BAGUETTE, A TASTY OMELETTE/OMELET AND AN ABUNDANCE OF CORIANDER/CILANTRO ARE ONE OF THE SIMPLEST BUT GREATEST OF PLEASURES. FOR AN EXTRA DIMENSION, DROP THE SLICED CHILLIES/CHILES INTO A BOWL OF GOOD SOY SAUCE AND BRUISE THEM WITH THE BACK OF A SPOON – THIS RELEASES THE CHILLIES/CHILES' FLAVOUR AND HEAT. DRIZZLE OVER THE BAGUETTE JUST BEFORE SERVING.

Mix all the pickle ingredients in a bowl and allow to rest for 15 minutes. Drain and wring with your hands.

For the omelette/omelet, beat the eggs in a bowl with the spring onions/scallions, sugar, salt, pepper and soy sauce. Heat the oil in a frying pan/skillet and briefly fry the shallots. Pour the egg mixture into the pan over the shallots and spread evenly. Cook for a couple of minutes until the underside looks golden brown (lift up one edge and check). Flip the omelette/omelet over and cook for a couple of minutes until brown. Remove from the heat and cut into strips.

To fill, slit the baguette lengthways and pull out the soft doughy inside (which can be used for breadcrumbs). Spread with butter and insert the omelette/omelet strips, pickle, coriander/cilantro and chillies.

Maple-cured BACON & TOMATO SANDWICH

THERE'S NO TURNING BACK ONCE YOU'VE TRIED HOMEMADE MAPLE-CURED BACON, ALTHOUGH YOU WILL NEED TO PREPARE IT A WEEK IN ADVANCE. WHEN IT'S READY, JUST TRY TO STOP YOURSELF FRYING UP THE WHOLE LOT AND WORKING YOUR WAY THROUGH IT WITH STICKY FINGERS AND GUILTY PLEASURE.

8 slices sourdough bread

2 tablespoons mayonnaise

4 eggs, cooked on both sides (optional)

8 tomato slices

4 slices Cheddar cheese (optional)

maple-cured bacon (see below), 2 slices per sandwich

a handful of rocket/arugula

sea salt and freshly ground black pepper

sweet pickles and sweet potato fries, to serve

Maple-cured bacon

140 g/1 cup sea salt

400 g/2 cups brown sugar (preferably soft dark brown sugar)

320 g/1 cup pure maple syrup

2.25–4.5 kg/5–10 lbs. pork belly, washed and patted dry, with the skin left on

SERVES 4

Curing bacon at home takes a while, but it's really worth it. In a medium bowl, combine the salt, sugar and maple syrup. Rub the mixture over the pork belly on both sides. Place the pork in a large resealable plastic bag with a zip and seal tightly. Refrigerate and let cure for 7 days, turning once a day.

After 7 days, the bacon will be cured. Cut off a small piece and fry it to test the saltiness of the bacon. If the bacon doesn't taste too salty after being cooked, you are ready to proceed. If the bacon tastes too salty, soak the remaining pork belly in cold water for 1 hour.

Once the bacon is ready to cook, carefully slice it into strips of the desired thickness. Fry it for 3–4 minutes per side, until it reaches the crispiness that you like. Fry the eggs, if using.

Assemble the sandwiches with slices of sourdough bread, mayonnaise, eggs (if using), tomatoes, Cheddar cheese (if using), rocket/arugula, salt and pepper. Serve with sweet pickles and sweet potato fries.

POSH FISH FINGER SANDWICH
& homemade tartare sauce

2 fillets of cod or haddock, skinned and boned

sunflower or vegetable oil, for frying

French country bread, to serve

butter, for spreading

a handful of cos/romaine lettuce leaves, cut into strips, to serve

fries, to serve

Beer batter

200 g/1½ cups plain/all-purpose flour

2 teaspoons sea salt

2 x 330-ml/11-fl. oz. bottles of lager

Homemade tartare sauce

225 g/1 cup mayonnaise

80 g/½ cup pickles/gherkins

1 teaspoon capers, chopped

2 teaspoons Dijon mustard

2 teaspoons chopped shallots

2 tablespoons chopped spring onions/scallions

2 teaspoons freshly squeezed lemon juice

Tabasco sauce to taste

sea salt and ground black pepper to taste

SERVES 2

THE POSH FISH FINGER SANDWICH IS ONE OF LONDON'S MOST FAMOUS DISHES. LAGER IS OFTEN USED IN THE BATTER FOR A RICHER FLAVOUR. HOMEMADE TARTARE SAUCE AND FRIES FINISH THE MEAL.

Prepare your fish for battering. Slice the fish into at least six finger-size strips.

For the batter, whisk the flour, salt and lager in a bowl until combined. Fill a large frying pan/skillet with about 2.5 cm/1 inch oil over high heat, but don't leave this unattended. When the oil is bubbling steadily, it's ready to go.

Dip the fish fingers in the batter, remove any excess and then lower carefully into the oil using tongs if necessary. Fry for about 4 minutes on each side over a moderate heat until golden and crispy.

Remove the fish fingers carefully from the oil and drain well on paper towels. Season with sea salt.

Mix all the ingredients for the tartare sauce together in a mixing bowl. Cut the French country bread into thick slices. Lay one down and butter it before spreading a couple of tablespoons of tartare sauce on top. Place 3 fish fingers on top, then a few strips of lettuce, before placing a second slice of bread on top. Serve with hand-cut fries.

Mac 'n' Cheese Sandwich

You can never have too much cheese in a grilled cheese sandwich but how to get it all in is the dilemma. The solution is to sneak it in on the back of something else, like mac 'n' cheese. This recipe is not for the health conscious but how much harm can just one sandwich do? It's best made with leftover mac 'n' cheese which is not too runny.

4 slices wholemeal/whole-
wheat sourdough bread

unsalted butter, softened

180 g/6½ oz. cooked
shredded ham hock

3–4 tablespoons spicy
barbecue sauce, to taste

160 g/2 cups
grated/shredded cheese,
such as Cheddar or
Monterey Jack

1–2 tablespoons sliced
pickled jalapeños
(optional)

2–4 big spoonfuls leftover
mac 'n' cheese

SERVES 2

Spread softened butter on the bread slices on one side.

In a small saucepan, combine the ham and barbecue sauce and cook over low heat, stirring, until warmed through. Set aside.

This is easiest if assembled in a large, heavy-based non-stick frying pan/skillet. Put two slices of bread in the frying pan/skillet, butter-side down. Top each bread slice with half of the cheese and half of the ham. It is best to drop the ham in spoonfuls and then spread the blobs out to the edges, gently, without disturbing the cheese beneath too much. Add jalapeños if using. Top this with blobs of mac 'n' cheese and spread gently to cover. Finally, top each one with a bread slice, this time butter-side up.

Turn the heat to medium and cook the first side for 5 minutes until deep golden, pressing gently with a spatula. Carefully turn each sandwich over with a large spatula and cook on the other side, for 2–3 minutes more or until deep golden brown all over.

Remove from the pan, transfer to plates and let cool for a few minutes before serving. Take care when eating as the filling will be hot.

Monte Cristo

2 eggs

4 tablespoons milk

4 slices white bread

unsalted butter, softened

4 slices or 250 g/scant 3 cups grated/shredded Emmental/Swiss cheese

2 slices ham, smoked or ordinary

icing/confectioners' sugar, to dust

strawberry jam/jelly, to serve

SERVES 2

THIS AMERICAN DINER STAPLE IS BASED ON THE CLASSIC FRENCH SNACK CROQUE-MONSIEUR – A GRILLED HAM AND CHEESE SANDWICH WITH BÉCHAMEL SAUCE. THIS VERSION IS MADE WITH FRENCH TOAST AND IS SERVED WITH JAM FOR A RETRO COMBINATION OF SWEET AND SAVOURY. SOME VERSIONS USE SLICED TURKEY AS WELL, WHICH IS JUST AS AUTHENTIC. YOU COULD EVEN TRY IT WITH A FRIED EGG ON TOP, LIKE A CROQUE-MADAME.

In a shallow dish, use a balloon whisk to beat together the eggs and milk. Set aside.

Lay two pieces of bread down on a clean work surface or chopping board and top them with one slice of cheese each, followed by a slice of ham and finally another slice of cheese. Top with the remaining bread slices to enclose both sandwiches.

Gently melt a large knob/pat of butter in a non-stick frying pan/skillet.

Meanwhile, working one at a time, carefully dip the sandwiches in the beaten egg mixture, turning to coat both sides.

Transfer the sandwiches to the hot frying pan/skillet and cook the first side for 3–5 minutes until deep golden. Depending on the size of your pan/skillet, you may need to cook one sandwich at a time. Carefully turn with a large spatula and cook on the second side for 2–3 minutes more or until golden brown all over.

Remove from the pan/skillet and transfer to a plate. Let cool for a few minutes, then dust with icing/confectioners' sugar, cut in half and serve with a little strawberry jam/jelly.

HOT BROWN

6 slices cold cooked turkey breast

4 slices grilled/broiled bacon, kept hot

a pinch of paprika, to garnish

fresh flat-leaf parsley, finely chopped, to garnish

Mornay sauce

40 g/3 tablespoons butter

40 g/⅓ cup plain/all-purpose flour

450 ml/scant 2 cups warmed milk (The Brown Hotel uses entirely double/heavy cream here; do it if you dare)

salt and freshly ground black pepper

115 g/1 cup grated/shredded Gruyère cheese, plus extra to garnish

Texas toast

a loaf of white bread

butter, at room temperature

SERVES 2

THE HOT BROWN IS LIKE CHEESE ON TOAST, WITH A ROCKET UP ITS BACKSIDE. CREATED BY FRED K. SCHMIDT AT THE BROWN HOTEL IN LOUISVILLE, KENTUCKY, IN 1926, IT IS AN OPEN SANDWICH PACKING SOME HEAVY WEIGHT, STARTING WITH "TEXAS TOAST," WHICH IS BREAD CUT TO TWICE THE THICKNESS OF REGULAR BREAD, THEN BUTTERED AND GRILLED/BROILED ON BOTH SIDES. IT IS TOPPED WITH SLICED TURKEY, CRISP BACON AND A VELVETEEN BLANKET OF MORNAY SAUCE.

To make the Mornay sauce, melt the butter in a saucepan, then mix in the flour, stirring well to form a thick paste (or roux). Cook this over a fairly gentle heat for a couple of minutes, stirring constantly and taking care not to colour the roux. Gradually whisk in the warmed milk and cook the sauce over medium heat until it comes to a boil – about 3 minutes. Reduce the heat to a simmer and season with salt and pepper. Whisk in the grated/shredded cheese until melted. Remove from the heat.

Preheat the grill/broiler to high.

Make the Texas toast by cutting four slices from the loaf of white bread to twice the thickness of regular slices, then buttering both sides and grilling/broiling each slice until crisp and golden on both sides.

To assemble, place a slice of Texas toast in each of two heatproof dishes. Top each with 3 slices of turkey breast and then pour some Mornay sauce over each. Sprinkle with extra cheese to garnish. Put under the hot grill/broiler until the cheese is melted and everything is bubbling.

Remove from the grill/broiler and top each with two slices of hot crispy bacon, then sprinkle with the paprika and parsley. Cut the remaining two slices of toast into triangles and serve around the outside of the sandwiches.

Mexican Torta

2 cooking chorizo sausages

2 tomatoes, diced

½ red onion, finely chopped

1 lime

1 teaspoon chipotle flakes, or 1 chipotle chilli/chile, finely chopped, or 1 fresh red chilli/chile, finely chopped

about 1 heaped tablespoon roughly chopped fresh coriander/cilantro

salt and freshly ground black pepper

1 avocado

2 Mexican rolls such as bolillo or telera, or 2 lengths of soft-ish white baguette, or 2 ciabatta rolls

2 tablespoons canned refried beans

MAKES 2

THE MEXICANS ARE VERY PROUD OF THEIR TORTAS. EVERY YEAR THEY PAY HOMAGE BY HOLDING A FESTIVAL IN MEXICO CITY; SUCH DEDICATION TO THE SANDWICH SHOULD BE ADMIRED. IT IS POSSIBLE THAT THE FIRST TORTA WAS EATEN DURING THE FRENCH OCCUPATION, WHEN MEXICANS TOOK INSPIRATION FROM THE BAGUETTE AND USED A SIMILAR RECIPE TO CREATE TELERA AND BOLILLO ROLLS. THEY'RE STUFFED WITH DIFFERENT COMBINATIONS OF INGREDIENTS DEPENDING ON THE REGION, BUT WHATEVER YOUR PREFERENCE, THE FILLINGS MUST BE MANY IN NUMBER. LAYER AND GARNISH TO YOUR HEART'S CONTENT. BUEN PROVECHO!

Set a frying pan/skillet or ridged griddle pan over a medium-high heat. Split the chorizo sausages in half lengthways, place them in the dry pan, cut-side down, and cook until crisp and beginning to char. Flip them over and cook the other side.

Meanwhile, make a tomato salsa by mixing the diced tomato and red onion with the juice of ½ a lime, the chipotle chilli/chile and coriander/cilantro. Season with salt and pepper. Halve, stone/pit stone and peel the avocado. In a separate bowl, mash the avocado and mix it with a squeeze of lime juice.

Cut the rolls in half and lightly toast them. Dip the cut-side of each roll into the chorizo pan to coat with some of the chorizo fat that has leached out during cooking. Spread one half of each roll with a layer of mashed avocado, then add the chorizo sausages. Top with the tomato salsa. Spread the other half of each roll with the refried beans and use them to top the sandwiches. Serve immediately.

Steak & Egg Breakfast Tacos

2 steaks

1–2 teaspoons olive oil, to season the steaks

8 eggs

8 small corn tortillas/tacos

vegetable oil, for shallow frying

tomato ketchup, for topping

salt and freshly ground black pepper

Serves 4

IT'S USUALLY THE BREAKFAST BURRITO THAT STEALS THE SHOW, BUT THESE STEAK AND EGG BREAKFAST TACOS ARE NOTHING TO SCOFF AT. FRIED EGGS, STEAK AND KETCHUP KEEP THIS DISH SIMPLE AND HEARTY.

To cook the steak, preheat the oven to 200ºC (400ºF) Gas 6 and heat a cast-iron skillet (or other heavy-bottomed and oven-safe pan) over medium heat.

Season the steaks with salt and pepper, using your fingers to rub the seasoning and about 1 teaspoon of olive oil into both sides of each steak. Add the steaks to the preheated pan and cook for 1–2 minutes on each side before sliding the pan into the preheated oven. Cook the steaks for a further 2–3 minutes for medium to medum-well done. Remove the pan from the oven and let the steaks rest for 2 minutes before slicing them into thin strips.

While the steaks rest, fry the eggs. Set a small non-stick frying pan/skillet over medium heat and add a little vegetable oil. Break in 1 egg. Season with a little salt and fry until the white is set. Remove to a warm plate and repeat with the remaining eggs.

If you can double-task, heat the tortillas, either by holding them directly over a gas flame with metal tongs, or in a cast-iron frying pan/skillet set over high heat. You want them to be puffed and a little blistered.

Place an egg on top of each tortilla and spoon the sliced steak on top of the egg. Top with ketchup and serve immediately.

4 small Cornish game hens
(Rock hen, Poussin, i.e.
small bird)

1 litre/4 cups buttermilk

1 large white onion, roughly
chopped

2 tablespoons chopped garlic

a bunch of fresh thyme sprigs

1–2 tablespoons hot sauce

4 litres/4 quarts canola or
peanut oil

4 whole garlic cloves, peeled

1 teaspoon salt

135 g/1 cup plain/all-purpose
flour

1 tablespoon cayenne pepper

45 g/1 cup panko
breadcrumbs

a pinch of paprika

Cornmeal Waffles

135 g/1 cup plain/
all-purpose flour

150 g/1 cup yellow
polenta/cornmeal

2 teaspoons baking powder

½ teaspoon bicarbonate of
soda/baking soda

¼ teaspoon salt

300 ml/2 cups buttermilk

2 eggs

115 g/1 stick unsalted butter,
melted and cooled slightly

non-stick spray, for greasing

4-litre/4-quart Dutch oven

kitchen twine

a waffle iron

SERVES 4

FRIED GAME HEN & CORNMEAL WAFFLES

HERE IS A VARIATION OF A MODERN CLASSIC BRUNCH DISH, FRIED CHICKEN AND WAFFLES. USING GAME HEN INSTEAD AND PAIRING IT WITH A MORE SAVOURY CORNMEAL WAFFLE, THIS RECIPE MAKES IT JUST A LITTLE MORE SUITABLE FOR BREAKFAST, BUT EVEN MORE SUITABLE FOR "BRINNER". THE GAME HEN REQUIRES A MINIMUM OF 6 HOURS TO MARINATE SO DON'T WAIT UNTIL YOU ARE HUNGRY TO START COOKING!

Remove any visible fat from the birds, rinse under cold water and pat dry. Combine the buttermilk, onion, garlic, eight of the thyme sprigs and the hot sauce together in a large bowl. Add the hens, turning to coat. Cover and marinate in the refrigerator for 6–12 hours.

Heat the oil in the Dutch oven fitted with a deep-fat thermometer over medium-high heat to 175°C (350°F). Remove the hens from the marinade and pat dry with paper towels. Place 1 garlic clove and the remaining thyme sprigs in each hen's cavity, tie the legs together with kitchen twine and sprinkle the hens with salt.

Whisk the flour and cayenne together in a medium bowl. Dredge the hens first in flour and then in panko, patting off excess flour. Fry 1 at a time for 10 minutes until crispy, golden brown and cooked through. Drain on a wire rack and let rest for 10 minutes while you prepare the waffles.

Preheat the oven to 110°C (200°F) to keep the waffles warm after they are cooked.

In a medium mixing bowl, whisk the dry ingredients together. In another bowl, mix the all the wet ingredients together, including the melted butter. Pour the wet into the dry and mix just until they are combined.

Lightly spray your waffle iron with non-stick spray and pour about 125 ml/½ cup batter for each waffle. Cook until browned and crisp. Place in oven to keep warm while cooking other waffles. Serve the warm hens with the waffles as soon as they are cooked.

Welsh Rarebit Waffles

200 g/1⅔ cups self-
raising/self-rising flour,
sifted

3 eggs, separated

250 ml/1 cup milk

75 g/⅓ cup butter, melted

sea salt and freshly ground
black pepper, to taste

Roasted tomatoes

300 g/1⅔ cups vine cherry
tomatoes

1–2 tablespoons olive oil

1 tablespoon balsamic glaze

1 tablespoon
caster/granulated sugar

Topping

300 g/3½ cups
grated/shredded Cheddar
cheese

1 egg

2 teaspoons wholegrain
mustard

1 tablespoon Worcestershire
sauce, plus extra to
splash

*an electric or stove-top
waffle iron*

SERVES 6

Welsh rarebit is so simple to prepare and makes a lovely supper, whether topping toast, a crumpet or, as in this recipe, a savoury waffle. Melted cheese with mustard and tangy Worcestershire sauce served with roasted vine tomatoes and a crisp green salad – what could be better?

Begin by preparing the tomatoes. Preheat the oven to 180°C (350°F) Gas 4.

Put the tomatoes in a roasting pan and drizzle with olive oil, the balsamic glaze and caster/granulated sugar. Season with salt and pepper and roast in the preheated oven for 20–30 minutes until the tomatoes are soft and their juices start to run. Keep warm until you are ready to serve.

To make the waffle batter, put the flour, egg yolks, milk and melted butter into a large mixing bowl. Whisk until you have a smooth batter. Season with salt and pepper. In a separate mixing bowl, whisk the egg whites to stiff peaks and then gently fold into the batter one-third at a time.

Preheat the waffle iron and grease with a little butter.

Ladle some of the batter into the preheated waffle iron and cook for 2–3 minutes until golden brown. Keep warm while you cook the remaining batter and are ready to serve.

For the topping, put all the ingredients into a bowl and mix.

Spread a large spoonful of the cheese mixture over each waffle and place under a hot grill/broiler for a few minutes until the cheese melts and starts to turn golden brown. Watch carefully to make sure that the rarebit topping and waffle do not burn, turning the grill/broiler heat down if required. Splash the tops of the waffles with a few drops of Worcestershire sauce and serve immediately with the roasted tomatoes on the side.

2–4 steaks

salt and freshly ground
black pepper

fresh coriander/cilantro,
to garnish

Waffle batter

5 cm/2 inch piece of fresh
ginger, peeled

260 g/2 cups self-raising/
self-rising flour, sifted

1 teaspoon baking powder

a pinch of salt

3 eggs, separated

375 ml/1½ cups milk

75 g/⅓ cup butter, melted,
plus extra for greasing

2 tablespoons finely
chopped fresh
coriander/cilantro

1 tablespoon sesame seeds

Dipping sauce

80 ml/scant ⅓ cup tamari
soy sauce

60 ml/¼ cup Worcestershire
sauce

60 ml/¼ cup maple syrup

1 heaped tablespoon tomato
ketchup

1 tablespoon olive oil

1 tablespoon sesame seeds

1 tablespoon freshly
chopped coriander/
cilantro

freshly ground black pepper

*an electric or stove-top
waffle iron*

SERVES 4

GINGER & SESAME WAFFLES
with steak & dipping sauce

**STEAK AND DIPPING SAUCE IS A CLASSIC. THESE STEAKS ARE SERVED
WITH DELICIOUS SESAME WAFFLES TO HELP MOP UP THE JUICES.**

To make the waffle batter, purée the ginger in a food processor, adding a little water if necessary. In a large mixing bowl, whisk together the flour, baking powder, salt, egg yolks, milk and melted butter until you have a smooth batter. Add the ginger purée, coriander/cilantro and sesame seeds and whisk again.

In a separate bowl, whisk the egg whites to stiff peaks. Gently fold the whisked egg whites into the batter mixture using a spatula.

Preheat the waffle iron and grease with a little butter.

Ladle some of the batter into the preheated waffle iron and cook for 2–3 minutes until golden brown. Keep the waffles warm while you cook the remaining batter and are ready to serve.

For the dipping sauce, put all of the ingredients in a bowl and whisk together well.

Season the steaks with salt and pepper and sear in a frying pan/skillet set over high heat. The cooking time will depend on how rare you like your meat. Sear for about 1–2 minutes on each side for rare and 3–4 minutes each side for well done, depending on the thickness of your steaks.

Slice the steaks very thinly and serve on top of two waffles per person with fresh coriander/cilantro and the dipping sauce on the side.

2 baking potatoes

260 g/2 cups self-raising/
　self-rising flour, sifted

1 teaspoon baking powder

a pinch of salt

3 eggs, separated

300 ml/1¼ cups milk

60 g/4 tablespoons butter,
　melted

a handful of grated/
　shredded Cheddar or
　Emmental/Swiss cheese,
　to serve

Barbecue beans

1 tablespoon olive oil

1 onion, peeled and finely
　sliced

1–2 garlic cloves, peeled
　and finely sliced

400 g/2 cups canned
　chopped tomatoes

2 tablespoons
　Worcestershire sauce

2 tablespoons soy sauce

40 g/¼ cup soft dark brown
　sugar

480 g/3¾ cups cooked
　cannellini beans, drained
　and rinsed

salt and freshly ground
　black pepper

*an electric or stove-top
　waffle iron*

*a baking sheet lined with
　baking parchment*

SERVES 4

POTATO WAFFLES
with barbecue beans

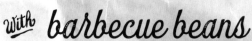

BARBECUE BEANS ARE AMONG THE TOP COMFORT FOODS. THEY ARE GREAT AS A SIDE DISH AND ARE REMINISCENT OF EVENINGS SPENT OPEN-AIR CAMPING, WITH SAUSAGES AND BEANS SIMMERING OVER GLOWING EMBERS. SERVED HERE WITH DELICIOUS POTATO WAFFLES, THIS RECIPE IS COMFORT FOOD HEAVEN.

Preheat the oven to 200°C (400°F) Gas 6.

Prick the potatoes with a fork and bake them in the preheated oven on the prepared baking sheet for 1 hour–1¼ hours (or in a microwave on full power for about 8 minutes per potato). Leave the potatoes to cool, then cut them open and remove the potato from the skins. Mash the flesh with a fork and discard the skins.

For the beans, heat the olive oil in a large saucepan or pot set over medium heat. Add the sliced onion and cook until they turn translucent. Add the garlic to the pan and cook for a few minutes longer until the onion and garlic are lightly golden brown. Add the tomatoes to the pan and season well with salt and pepper. Add the Worcestershire sauce, soy sauce and dark brown sugar and simmer until the sauce becomes thick and syrupy. Put the beans in the sauce and simmer for a further 20 minutes. Keep the pan on the heat but turn it down to low to keep the beans warm until you are ready to serve.

In a large mixing bowl, whisk together the cooled mashed potato, flour, baking powder, salt, egg yolks, milk and melted butter until you have a smooth batter. In a separate bowl, whisk the egg white to stiff peaks. Gently fold the whisked egg whites into the batter mixture using a spatula.

Preheat the waffle iron and grease with a little butter.

Ladle some of the batter into the preheated waffle iron and cook for 3–5 minutes until golden brown. Keep the waffles warm while you cook the remaining batter.

Serve the waffles topped with the hot barbecue beans and grated/shredded cheese.

Huevos Rancheros Waffle

160 g/1⅓ cups self-raising/rising flour, sifted

100 g/1 cup fine yellow cornmeal/polenta

1 teaspoon bicarbonate of soda/baking soda

1 tablespoon caster/granulated sugar

3 eggs, separated

375 ml/1½ cups milk

60 g/¼ cup butter, melted

Salsa

4 large tomatoes, halved

2 ripe avocados

freshly squeezed juice of 2 limes

2 heaped tablespoons finely chopped fresh coriander/cilantro

½ teaspoon hot paprika, plus extra for dusting

sea salt and freshly ground black pepper

Topping

1 tablespoon olive or vegetable oil

8 eggs

70 g/scant 1 cup Cheddar cheese, grated

sour cream, to serve

sea salt and freshly ground black pepper

an electric or stove-top waffle iron

SERVES 4

Huevos Rancheros or "ranch eggs" are a traditional Mexican breakfast of spicy tomatoes with eggs served on corn tortillas. This version uses corn waffles in place of the tortillas. Although the tomatoes are traditionally cooked, the tomato and avocado salsa used here is much fresher. The kick of piquant paprika and the delicate fragrance of coriander will wake up your senses in the morning, but they also combine to make a warming dinner option.

First, make the salsa. Remove the seeds from the halved tomatoes using a teaspoon and discard. Cut the hollowed out tomatoes into small pieces using a sharp knife. Prepare the avocado by removing the stones and skins and cutting the flesh into small pieces. Immediately mix the avocado with the lime juice and tomatoes so that it does not discolour. Add the coriander/cilantro, sprinkle over the paprika and stir in. Season with salt and pepper and set aside in the refrigerator until needed.

To make the waffle batter, put the flour, cornmeal/polenta, bicarbonate of soda/baking soda, caster/granulated sugar, egg yolks, milk and melted butter in a large mixing bowl. Whisk until you have a smooth batter. Season with salt and pepper. In a separate mixing bowl, whisk the egg whites to stiff peaks and then gently fold into the batter one-third at a time.

Preheat the waffle iron and grease with a little butter. Ladle some of the batter into the preheated waffle iron and cook for 2–3 minutes until golden brown. Keep the waffles warm while you cook the remaining batter and are ready to serve.

For the topping, heat the oil in a frying pan/skillet and fry the 8 eggs for 2–3 minutes until the whites of the eggs are cooked but the yolks are still soft and runny.

Place the waffles on plates and top each with a generous portion of the salsa. Place the fried eggs on top and sprinkle over the grated cheese. Top with a spoonful of sour cream and a pinch of paprika, and serve straight away.

PORK SAUSAGE & LEEK WAFFLE *with* split pea "syrup"

THIS SAUSAGE AND LEEK WAFFLE IS A SAVOURY TAKE ON ONE OF THE WORLD'S MOST BELOVED BREAKFAST ITEMS. ADD SAUSAGE AND LEEK TO TAKE THIS BASIC BUTTERMILK RECIPE FROM MORNING TO NIGHT. SERVE ALONGSIDE A SPLIT PEA "SYRUP", WHICH ESSENTIALLY IS REALLY NOT A SYRUP, BUT A SPLIT PEA PURÉE.

1 large russet potato, pricked with a fork

½ tablespoon vegetable oil

1 large leek, white and light green parts sliced and rinsed

125 ml/½ cup full-fat/whole milk

2 tablespoons sour cream

2 eggs

20 g/¼ cup coarsely grated Parmesan cheese

40 g/¼ cup plain/all-purpose flour

2½ teaspoons baking powder

225 g/½ lb. pork sausage, cooked and crumbled (reserve the fat and set aside)

salt and ground white pepper

non-stick spray, for greasing

Split pea "syrup"

225 g/1¼ cups green split peas

1 onion, peeled, sliced

1 leek, white part only, sliced

1 teaspoon dried mint, crushed

1 teaspoon dried marjoram, crushed

½ teaspoon salt

¼–½ teaspoon freshly ground black pepper

1 tablespoon white vinegar

3 tablespoons butter mixed with reserved sausage drippings

a waffle iron

SERVES 4

Preheat the oven to 200ºC (400ºF) Gas 6.

Bake the potato in the preheated oven until soft, about 1 hour, turning once halfway through.

Meanwhile, make the split pea "syrup". Fill a large saucepan with 500 ml/2 cups water. Add the split peas, onion, leek, mint, marjoram, salt and pepper. Simmer on low until peas and onion are very tender, about 45 minutes. Remove from the heat and let cool slightly. Add the vinegar and purée in two batches in a blender or food processor. Transfer to a saucepan or pot and set aside.

Once the baked potato is cooked, scoop the cooked flesh out of the potato into a medium bowl and mash. Set aside. Discard the skin.

Heat the vegetable oil in a small frying pan/skillet over medium heat. Add the leeks and sauté until softened but not browned, about 4 minutes. Season with salt and pepper. Remove from the heat.

Add the leeks, sour cream and milk to the potato and whisk together. Whisk in the eggs and cheese. Whisk in the flour and baking powder until a thick batter is formed. Let rest.

Heat a waffle iron and coat with non-stick spray. Pour the batter into the waffle iron and top with the crumbled, cooked sausage. Cook until lightly browned. Keep warm in a low oven while other waffles cook. Reheat the split pea purée.

Serve the warm waffles with the split pea purée poured over, or serve it alongside to dip.

Skillet suppers

Spiced Pulled Pork Hash

400 g/14-oz. sweet potatoes, peeled

2 tablespoons vegetable oil

2 tablespoons butter

1 red onion, chopped

⅛-¼ teaspoon cayenne pepper, to taste

salt and freshly ground black pepper, to taste

Pulled pork

700-g/1½-lb. boneless pork shoulder/butt

1 tablespoon caraway seeds

2 whole cloves

1 star anise

½ tablespoon whole black peppercorns

100 g/½ cup coarse sea salt

SERVES 4

MIX ROASTED SWEET POTATOES AND MELT-IN-THE-MOUTH PULLED PORK FOR A TASTY TAKE ON HASH. THE SPICY MIX OF SEASONING HERE WITH THE TENDER PULLED PORK WILL MELT IN YOUR MOUTH. THE PORK WILL TAKE 4–5 HOURS TO COOK, SO YOU NEED TO START THIS RECIPE IN THE MORNING OR COOK THE PORK THE DAY BEFORE. ANY LEFTOVER MEAT CAN BE USED IN THE CHEDDAR HOTCAKES RECIPE ON PAGE 106.

Preheat the oven to 120°C (250°F) Gas 4.

First, prepare the pulled pork. Combine the caraway seeds, cloves, star anise and peppercorns in a mortar and grind with a pestle or use an electric spice grinder. Crush or process until ground and with the same texture as the coarse salt. Mix the ground spices with the salt. Firmly rub the spice rub into the pork shoulder/butt until it is all used up and the meat is completely covered. Place the pork in a roasting pan and cover tightly with kitchen foil. Cook in the preheated oven for 4–5 hours, turning once or twice during this time. When ready, the meat will be tender enough for you to pull it into shreds using two forks.

Meanwhile, cut the sweet potatoes into small 0.5-cm/1.4-inch cubes. Heat the oil to a frying pan/skillet and when hot, add the sweet potato cubes. Stir-fry for about 10 minutes until cooked through. Set aside until needed. When you are ready to cook the hash, melt the butter in a frying pan/skillet over medium heat. Add the onion and cook until slightly softened, about 2 minutes. Add the shredded spicy pork and continue to cook for 2 minutes more.

Stir the cooked sweet potatoes into the pork and onion mixture and toss. Cook, stirring occasionally, about 5 minutes, until everything is piping hot. Season to taste with the salt, black pepper and cayenne pepper and serve immediately.

TEX-MEX SKILLET

1 tablespoon olive oil

1 large brown or red onion, finely chopped

1 teaspoon ground cumin

2 teaspoons chilli/chili powder

a pinch of chilli flakes/hot red pepper flakes

2 large garlic cloves, finely chopped

225 g/8 oz. minced/ground beef

2 courgettes/zucchini, cut into large cubes

145 g/1 cup uncooked corn kernels (shucked fresh off the cob or frozen)

425 g/1½ cups cooked black beans, drained

about 15 black olives, pitted and sliced

about 5 whole pickled Jalapeños, sliced, or 3 tablespoons sliced

1 tablespoon tomato purée/paste

freshly squeezed juice of 1 lemon

1 teaspoon salt

75 g/generous ¾ cup grated/shredded mature/sharp Cheddar cheese

tortilla chips or corn tortillas, to serve

SERVES 4

GET YOUR ALMOST-SOUTH-OF-THE-BORDER FIX WITH THIS GREAT SOUTHWEST TEX-MEX SKILLET. IT'S A LITTLE BIT SOUTHERN AND A LITTLE BIT MEXICAN. SERVE WITH TORTILLAS.

Preheat the grill/broiler to high.

Heat the oil in a 25-cm/10-inch frying pan/skillet over medium heat. Add the onion, cumin, chilli/chili powder and chilli flakes/hot red pepper flakes and sauté until nearly tender, about 4–5 minutes.

Add the garlic and sauté for another minute. Add the minced/ground beef and scramble until nearly cooked through (though still slightly pink). Add the courgette/zucchini and corn. Sauté until just barely tender, but not soft.

Remove from the heat and stir in the black beans, olives, jalapeños, tomato purée/paste, lemon juice and salt. Taste and add more salt or additional chilli/chili powder or chilli flakes/hot red pepper flakes to taste. Remove from the heat.

Sprinkle the cheese over the surface of the mixture and set under the hot grill/broiler until melted and bubbly. Serve immediately with tortilla chips or warm corn tortillas.

Caprese Skillet

2 tablespoons olive oil

½ white onion, finely chopped

3 tomatoes, thinly sliced

½ teaspoon salt

½ teaspoon black pepper

4 eggs

200 g/1½ cups grated/shredded firm mozzarella cheese

a handful of fresh Basil leaves

cracked black pepper, to serve

good-quality balsamic vinegar, to drizzle (optional)

4 slices of ciabatta/Italian bread, toasted, to serve

SERVES 4

THIS SKILLET IS A GREAT COMBINATION OF A CLASSIC ITALIAN INSALATA CAPRESE (A SUBLIMELY SIMPLE COMBINATION OF MOZZARELLA, TOMATO AND FRESH BASIL) AND EGGS. THE TOMATOES WILL BE A LITTLE MORE LIQUEFIED THAN MANY SKILLETS, BUT THE BREAD IS THERE TO SOAK UP ALL THOSE DELICIOUS JUICES! DRIZZLE WITH A GOOD AGED BALSAMIC VINEGAR FOR A LITTLE EXTRA ZING.

Heat the olive oil in a medium-large frying pan/skillet set over medium heat and sauté the onion until softened. Add the tomatoes, salt and pepper and continue to cook until the tomatoes begin to soften and release their juices, about 5 minutes.

Use a large spoon to create 4 evenly spaced depressions in the tomato mixture. Crack an egg in each depression, cover the frying pan/skillet and cook until the whites have set and the yolks are almost cooked to desired doneness, 3–4 minutes.

Sprinkle the cheese over the top, cover with a lid and cook just until the cheese is melted. Scatter over the basil and cracked black pepper and serve with the toasted bread on the side.

Spinach, Artichoke & Goats' Cheese Pizza

1 pizza base (see recipe below), unbaked

125 ml/½ cup Simple Tomato Sauce (see page 76)

250 g/2 cups firm mozzarella, grated

400g/14-oz. can quartered artichoke hearts, drained and halved

60–90 g/2–3 cups fresh baby spinach leaves, destalked

1 large ripe tomato, cut into large chunks

60 g/½ cup small balls or sliced rounds of soft white goats' cheese

a large handful of fresh basil leaves

chilli flakes/hot red pepper flakes, to taste (optional)

Pizza base

7 g/¼ oz. packet active dry yeast

1 teaspoon white sugar

250 ml/1 cup warm water (110°F/45°C)

340 g/2½ cups strong white/bread flour

2 tablespoons olive oil

1 teaspoon salt

polenta/cornmeal, for dusting

a pizza pan, lightly greased or pizza peel or stone

SERVES 2–4

THIS PIZZA HAS A MIXTURE OF GREEN VEGETABLES AND MILD CREAMY GOATS' CHEESE THAT MAKE IT A DELICIOUS AND MASTERFUL WAY OF ENJOYING PIZZA THAT IS BOTH PACKED WITH FLAVOUR YET LIGHT, FRESH AND NUTRITIOUS. VIRTUOUS COMFORT FOOD – WHAT'S NOT TO LIKE?

Start by making the pizza base. Preheat the oven to 230°C (450°F) Gas 8.

In a medium bowl, dissolve the yeast and sugar in the warm water. Let stand until creamy, about 10 minutes.

Stir in the flour, oil and salt. Beat until smooth, then let rest for 5 minutes.

Turn the dough out onto a lightly floured surface and pat or roll into a round of about 30 cm/12 inches. Transfer the crust to the lightly greased pizza pan or onto a baker's peel dusted with polenta/cornmeal.

Spread the tomato sauce on the crust. Sprinkle half of the mozzarella over the tomato sauce. Scatter spinach leaves evenly over the crust then top with the artichokes and tomato slices Sprinkle the remaining mozzarella cheese on top (the cheese will hold it together).

Arrange small balls/slices of goat cheese over the top and add some torn fresh basil to the top of the pizza. Crack an egg on top (trying to not break the yolk), if using.

Bake in the preheated oven for 15–20 minutes, or until golden brown. Let the baked pizza cool for 5 minutes. Sprinkle some chilli flakes/hot red pepper flakes over the top, if using, and serve immediately.

CHICAGO STRATA

12 eggs

250 ml/1 cup milk or single/light cream

900 g/2 lb. slightly stale hot dog buns, cut into cubes or torn into pieces

90 g/1 cup grated/shredded Cheddar cheese

4 cooked hot dogs or Polish sausages, chopped

2–3 teaspoons olive oil

1 large white onion, chopped

3 dill pickle spears (or 1 large whole dill pickle), chopped

400-g/14-oz can chopped tomatoes, well drained or 8–12 sundried/sunblush tomatoes, cut into pieces

a 23 x 33-cm/9 x 13-inch baking dish, well buttered

SERVES 4

BY DEFINITION, A STRATA IS A BREAKFAST "CASSEROLE" MADE WITH MEAT, BREAD, EGGS AND HERBS. THIS STRATA IS A HOMAGE TO MY HOMETOWN, CHICAGO. IT'S ESSENTIALLY A DECONSTRUCTED CHICAGO HOT DOG. USING STALE HOT DOG BUNS INSTEAD OF BREAD AND REPLACING SAUSAGE OR HAM WITH FRANKFURTERS, IT'S A DISH THAT CAN BE SERVED ANY TIME OF DAY. PAIR ALONG WITH A SALAD OR STEAK FRIES AND TOP WITH KETCHUP, MUSTARD AND SAUERKRAUT.

Preheat the oven to 180°C (350°F) Gas 4.

Crack 7 of the eggs into a bowl and beat. Add the milk or cream and beat to combine.

Spread the hot dog bun cubes over the bottom of the buttered dish. Pour the egg and milk mixture over the bun cubes and stir to coat. Let it sit for 20 minutes for the mixture to soak into the bread. You can also soak the milk and bun cubes overnight for a lighter texture.

Meanwhile, heat the oil in a frying pan/skillet and sauté the onion until translucent. Remove from the pan and set aside. Add the pickles to the pan and sauté for about 3 minutes, until softened. Set aside.

Sprinkle half of the cheese over the soaked bun cubes. Add the sautéed onions and pickles. Add the cooked hot dogs or Polish sausage. Add the tomatoes. Layer with the remaining cheese. Beat the remaining 5 eggs and pour over the top of the strata.

Bake in the preheated oven for 45 minutes. Serve hot with a crisp leaf salad or steak fries, as preferred.

Triple Meat & Cheddar Breakfast Quiche

Filling

4 slices streaky/fatty bacon

2 pork sausages

6 eggs, well beaten

125 ml/½ cup full-fat/ whole milk

¼ teaspoon salt

a pinch of ground black pepper

60 g/½ cup chopped lean ham

2 large spring onions/ scallions, sliced

90 g/1 cup grated/shredded Cheddar cheese

Pie crust dough

130 g/1 cup plain/all-purpose flour

½ teaspoon salt

60 ml/¼ cup olive oil

60 ml/¼ cup iced water

a 23-cm/9-inch tart pan, lightly greased

MAKES 1 QUICHE

THIS IS THE ULTIMATE QUICHE FOR MEAT-LOVERS! IT IS FILLED WITH SAUSAGE, BACON AND HAM – THE TRINITY OF BREAKFAST MEATS – AND MIXED WITH EGGS AND MILK FOR A FLUFFY AND HEARTY (BUT NOT TOO HEAVY) MEAL. THE FLAKY PIE CRUST GIVES THIS DISH AMAZING TEXTURE. IT'S EQUALLY DELICIOUS SERVED WARM OR COLD.

To make the pie crust, put the flour and salt in a mixing bowl and stir with a fork to combine. Beat the oil and water together with a small whisk or fork until emulsified. Pour the water and oil mixture into the flour and mix with a fork. Roll the dough into a ball, wrap in cling film/plastic wrap and refrigerate for at least 30 minutes before using.

To prepare the quiche filling, cook the bacon in a dry frying pan/skillet until crisp. Remove from the pan and set aside. Remove the skins from the sausages and add the sausage meat to the pan. Cook it over medium-high heat, breaking it up with a wooden spoon, until cooked through. Crumble the cooked bacon and set the crumbled bacon and sausage aside.

Preheat the oven to 220°C (425°F) Gas 7. Roll out the chilled pastry/pie dough and press it into the prepared tart pan. Prick the base with a fork and bake in the preheated oven for about 10 minutes, until lightly browned.

In a large bowl, whisk together the eggs, milk, salt and pepper. Arrange the cooked bacon, sausagemeat and ham in the part-baked pie crust and evenly sprinkle the spring onions/ scallions and cheese over the top. Carefully pour the egg mixture on top, taking care not to overfill the pie crust.

Bake the quiche in the preheated oven for about 20–25 minutes, until the filling is set in the centre and a cocktail stick/toothpick comes out clean. Allow to cool slightly before serving.

"Pizza Pie" Quiche

2 quantities Pie Crust Dough (see page 75), chilled

3 eggs

225 g/1 cup ricotta cheese

1 teaspoon Italian seasoning

225 g/8 oz. spicy Italian sausage, cooked and chopped

350 ml/1½ cups Simple Tomato Sauce (see below)

115 g/1 cup grated/shredded mozzarella cheese

about 20 slices pepperoni, chopped

40 g/½ cup grated/shredded Parmesan cheese

melted butter, for brushing

Simple tomato sauce

400-g/14-oz jar of tomato passata/strained tomatoes

1½ teaspoons crushed/minced garlic

1 tablespoon dried oregano

1 teaspoon ground paprika

salt and freshly ground black pepper

a 23-cm/9-inch tart pan, lightly greased

SERVES 2–4

PIZZA AND EGGS DON'T TRADITIONALLY SOUND LIKE THEY'D BE A GOOD COMBINATION – UNTIL YOU MAKE THIS QUICHE. HALF PIZZA PIE, HALF CHEESE QUICHE AND A WHOLE LOT OF DELICIOUS!

Preheat the oven to 220°C (425°F) Gas 7.

Roll out two thirds of the chilled pastry/pie dough and press it into the tart pan, prick the base with a fork and bake in the preheated oven until lightly browned, about 10 minutes. (Return the remaining dough to the fridge until needed.) Remove from the oven and reduce the oven temperature to 175°C (350°F) Gas 4.

Meanwhile, to make the simple pizza sauce, heat the passata in a small saucepan with the other sauce ingredients. Bring to the boil, reduce the heat and let simmer for 5 minutes. Season to taste with salt and pepper. To make the filling, combine the eggs, ricotta cheese and Italian seasoning in a bowl and beat well. Stir in the cooked sausage, 175 ml/¾ cup of the pizza sauce, mozzarella cheese, pepperoni and Parmesan cheese. Spoon the egg mixture into the part-baked pastry case/pie crust.

Roll out the remaining pastry. Cut a 20-cm/8-inch circle out of the remaining pastry. Cut the circle into 6 triangles. Arrange these on top of filling to resemble pizza slices, brush with melted butter and return to the oven for 45–50 minutes until golden brown. Spoon a little of the remaining pizza sauce over each 'pizza slice' and let cool for 10 minutes before serving.

Chorizo Breakfast Nacho Skillet
with homemade tortilla chips

WHAT CAN BE SAID ABOUT BREAKFAST NACHOS? THEY ARE PERFECT FOR ANY TIME OF DAY. USING SPICY CHORIZO SAUSAGE, SCRAMBLED EGG AND A BLEND OF THREE CHEESES, THIS RECIPE EASILY TRANSITIONS FROM BREAKFAST TO DINNER. THE TEXTURES ARE FANTASTIC AND THE DISH HAS PLENTY OF SPICY MEXICAN FLAIR.

450 g/1 lb. chorizo sausage

½ white onion, chopped

5 eggs, beaten

4 ripe tomatoes, chopped

2 jarred jalapeño peppers, sliced

225 g/8 oz. pre-packaged "Mexican blend" grated/shredded cheese or a mixture of freshly grated/shredded mature/sharp Cheddar, mild Cheddar/Colby and Gouda/Monterey Jack

125 ml/½ cup sour cream

Homemade tortilla chips

1 packet soft flour or corn tortillas, as preferred

2 tablespoons vegetable oil

a baking sheet, lightly greased

a cast-iron frying pan/skillet

SERVES 4

Preheat the oven to 180°C (350°F) Gas 4.

First make the tortilla chips. With a pastry brush or turkey basting brush, paint a very light coating of oil on one side of each tortilla. Stack the tortillas greased side up in an even pile. Divide the stack in two and cut the tortillas into quarters and then into eighths. Separate the chips and arrange them greased-side up on the prepared baking sheet.

Bake the chips in the preheated oven for about 10 minutes or until they are crisp and just beginning to brown slightly. Remove them from the oven but you can leave the oven on if you are ready to make up the frying pan/skillet.

Cook the chorizo in a frying pan/skillet over medium heat until crumbled and evenly browned, about 5 minutes. Drain and set aside. Cook the onion in the same frying pan/skillet until soft, then stir in the eggs and scramble with the onion. Mix in the tomatoes and continue to cook and stir until the eggs are nearly set. Remove from the heat.

Spread a layer of tortilla chips into a medium cast-iron frying pan/skillet. Scatter the chorizo and the scrambled egg mixture over the chips. Top with jalapeño slices and cover with the grated/shredded cheese.

Bake in the preheated oven for 7–10 minutes, until the cheese is melted. Serve hot and eat with your fingers!

DEVILLED BUBBLE & SQUEAK

25 g/2 tablespoons butter

1 large onion, finely chopped

1 garlic clove, crushed (optional)

1 large cooked potato (about 250 g/8½ oz.), cubed or roughly mashed

150 g/5 oz. cooked Brussels sprouts, finely chopped

50 g/½ cup cooked, shredded cabbage or other leafy green vegetable

a handful of frozen peas (optional)

1 tablespoon hot chilli/chile sauce (your favourite!)

1 tablespoon Worcestershire sauce

salt and freshly ground black pepper

SERVES 2

PART OF BEING A GOOD COOK IS BEING ABLE TO MAKE SOMETHING INVITING FROM THE INGREDIENTS YOU HAVE TO HAND. ENGLISH "BUBBLE AND SQUEAK" IN ANY OF ITS VARIATIONS HELPS YOU DO THAT WONDERFULLY WELL. IT IS A TRUE COMFORT FOOD. THE RESULTS ARE TASTY AND FILLING AND IT ESSENTIALLY USES BITS AND PIECES THAT MAY OTHERWISE HAVE BEEN THROWN AWAY, ALTHOUGH TRADITIONALLY IT IS MADE WITH LEFTOVER CABBAGE AND POTATO.

Melt the butter in a frying pan/skillet over medium heat and gently fry the onion for 2–3 minutes. Increase the heat slightly and add the garlic and potato. Fry for another 2 minutes, or until the onion and garlic have softened.

Add the Brussels sprouts, cabbage, peas, if using, chilli/chile sauce and Worcestershire sauce. Continue cooking for a further 8–10 minutes, turning everything two or three times to ensure it is heating through but allowing the potato to brown. Season with salt and pepper.

Serve the bubble and squeak with a fried egg on top for a hearty breakfast. You might also want to splash some extra chilli/chile sauce on top!

Tip: This recipe can be altered to include whatever leftover vegetables you have to hand. As a general rule, though, it needs to have potato in some form and some kind of green, leafy veg. Apart from that, the only rule is that there are none.

Cajun-spiced, SOUFFLÉD BAKED POTATOES

2 large baking potatoes, scrubbed

a large knob/pat of butter

1 big teaspoon Dijon mustard

2 teaspoons Cajun spice blend

2 spring onions/scallions, chopped

1 mild green chilli/chile, deseeded and chopped

100 g/1 cup grated/shredded mature/sharp Cheddar, plus extra for sprinkling

1 egg, lightly beaten

salt and freshly ground black pepper

SERVES 2

HERE IS A TASTY WAY OF EMBELLISHING THIS HUMBLE DISH. THE POSSIBLE VARIATIONS ARE ENDLESS: WITH THE ADDITION OF A LEAFY GREEN SALAD IT IS QUITE EASY TO TURN IT INTO AN ENTIRE MEAL OR YOU CAN KEEP IT SIMPLE AND SERVE AS AN INTRIGUING ACCOMPANIMENT FOR YOUR MAIN MEAL.

Preheat the oven to 200°C (400°F) Gas 6.

Pierce the potato skins several times with a fork, then place the potatoes directly on a shelf in the preheated oven. Bake until the flesh is soft enough to scrape out, and the skins are crispy enough to retain their shape – about 50–70 minutes, depending on the size of the potatoes. Leave the oven on.

Once the potatoes are soft, let them cool slightly until they are cool enough to handle. Cut them in half lengthways and carefully spoon the insides into a large bowl. Mash the potato until it is fairly lump-free, then add the butter, mustard, Cajun spice blend, spring onions/scallions, chilli/chile and cheese. (Reserve a couple of pieces of chilli/chile to decorate the tops of the potatoes if you like.) Stir together until well mixed. Check the seasoning – the Cajun spice blend will contain a fair amount of salt, so do taste it before you add too much more. When you are satisfied that the seasoning is right, quickly mix the beaten egg through the mashed potato mixture and then spoon the mixture back into the skins.

Sprinkle some extra grated/shredded cheese over the filled potatoes and top with the reserved chilli/chile pieces, if using. Place the potatoes into a small baking dish and return to the oven for a further 15–20 minutes or until the cheese starts to brown. The egg will cause the potatoes to rise slightly in a sort of scaled-down soufflé effect, giving them an unexpected lightness.

Serve with a tasty mixed salad and simple piece of grilled/broiled fish or chicken.

Tip: For a tempting and easy supper, add a can of tuna to the potatoes when you mix in the other ingredients.

Leek and sausage hash browns

- 1 tablespoon olive oil
- 12 chipolata sausages
- 6 medium potatoes, peeled, cooked and diced
- 350 g/12 oz. leeks, sliced and cooked
- 1 tablespoon horseradish sauce, or more to taste
- 100 g/1 scant cup grated/ shredded Gruyère cheese
- salt and freshly ground black pepper

Steak and potato hash browns

- 2 tablespoons canola oil
- 1 large green (bell) pepper, chopped
- 1 small onion, chopped
- 3 medium potatoes, peeled, cooked and chopped
- 1 steak, cooked and chopped
- ½ teaspoon garlic powder
- 30 g/¼ cup grated/ shredded Swiss cheese
- 4 eggs
- salt and freshly ground black pepper

Tater Tots

- 8 medium potatoes
- 1 tablespoon plain/ all-purpose flour
- 2 tablespoons very finely chopped white onions
- vegetable oil, for frying
- salt and freshly ground black pepper

HASH BROWNS THREE WAYS

HASH BROWNS ARE ONE OF THE WORLD'S BEST SIDES. THESE THREE RECIPES ALL SERVE 4 AND SPRUCE UP THE REGULAR OLD POTATO, SALT AND PEPPER MIX. LEEK AND SAUSAGE BRINGS A SEASONAL TASTE, WHILE STEAK POTATOES ARE THE PERFECT SKILLET SUPPER. TATOR TOTS ARE BITE-SIZE HASH BROWNS. DIP THEM IN KETCHUP AND SERVE THEM HOT WITH ANY MAIN TO MAKE KIDS EXCITED AND ADULTS NOSTALGIC.

Leek and Sausage Hash Browns

Heat the oil in a large frying pan/skillet over medium heat. Add the sausages and fry for 8-10 minutes until well browned and cooked through. Remove the sausages, then slice them on the diagonal and set aside.

Turn the heat to high, then add the potatoes and leeks and give them a good stir. Continue to cook on a fairly high heat until the potatoes begin to brown and turn crisp.

Toss the sausage slices back in along with the creamed horseradish and cook for a further 2–3 minutes. Take the pan off the heat, sprinkle in the cheese, season well and gently stir to combine

Steak and Potato Hash Browns

Heat the oil in a large frying pan/skillet and sauté the green (bell) pepper and onion until tender. Stir in the potatoes.

Reduce the heat, cover and cook over low heat for 10 minutes or until the potatoes are heated through, stirring occasionally.

Add the cooked steak and garlic powder and season well. Sprinkle with cheese. Cover and cook over low heat for 5 minutes more or until heated through and cheese is melted. Keep warm.

Prepare the eggs as desired, either fried or poached is perfect. Divide the hash among four serving plates and top each one with an egg. Serve immediately.

Tater Tots (pictured left)

Cook the potatoes, unpeeled, in a pan of boiling water until tender. As soon as they are cool enough to handle, peel them and then finely grate/shred them or use a ricer. Stir in the flour, 1 teaspoon of salt, a pinch of black pepper and the chopped onion

Heat 5 mm/¼ inch of the oil for frying in a heavy-bottomed pan.

Form the potato mixture into small balls. Carefully drop the potato balls into the hot oil, in batches, and fry until slightly golden. Remove with a slotted spoon and drain on paper towels. Serve immediately.

Brinner in a bowl

SHIO RAMEN
with pork & eggs

1 tablespoon sake

1 tablespoon mirin

1 garlic clove, crushed

1 teaspoon freshly
grated/shredded ginger

50 ml/¼ cup dark soy sauce

50 ml/¼ cup light soy sauce

1 tablespoon
caster/granulated sugar

750 g/1½ lb. piece of pork
belly, skin removed

4 eggs

2 litres/2 quarts chicken
stock

250 g/9 oz. dried ramen
noodles

spring onions/scallions,
thinly sliced to garnish

SERVES 4

SHIO RAMEN IS A SALTY RAMEN NOODLE SOUP THAT IS QUITE LIGHT IN FLAVOUR AND COLOUR MAKING IT A CLASSIC START TO THE DAY IN JAPAN. THE PORK BELLY AND EGGS HERE TRANSFORM THIS INTO A TASTY AND SATISFYING BREAKFAST FOR DINNER BOWL.

Pour the sake and mirin into a small saucepan set over medium heat and bring slowly to the boil. Add the garlic, ginger, dark and light soy sauces and the sugar, and stir until the sugar dissolves. Bring to the boil and simmer very gently for 5 minutes. Remove from the heat and leave to cool.

Cut the pork belly in half across the grain to make two similar squares and put in a saucepan into which the pork fits snugly.

Pour over the cooled soy mixture, return to the heat and bring to the boil. Cover and simmer gently for 1 hour or until the pork is tender. Remove the pan from the heat but leave the pork in the stock to cool at room temperature. Remove the pork from the stock, reserving the stock, and cut into thick slices. Set aside.

Put the eggs in a saucepan of cold water and set over high heat. Bring to the boil and simmer for 5 minutes. Remove the eggs from the pan and immediately rinse under cold running water until they are cool enough to handle. Peel the eggs and place them in a clean bowl. Pour over the reserved pork stock and leave to soak for 30 minutes. Lift the eggs from the stock and cut in half lengthways.

Meanwhile bring the chicken stock to the boil in a large saucepan and simmer until reduced by about one-third to 1.25 litres/5 cups. Remove from the heat and stir in 4 tablespoons of the reserved pork stock. Add the pork belly slices and warm through for 5 minutes.

Plunge the noodles into a saucepan of boiling water, return to the boil and cook for about 4 minutes or until al dente. Drain well, then divide the noodles between soup bowls. Spoon over the stock and pork slices, add two egg halves to each bowl and serve garnished with spring onions/scallions.

SHRIMP & GRITS
with tomato sauce & turkey sausage

GRITS ARE A TRADITIONAL AMERICAN DISH MADE WITH GROUND DRIED HOMINY (PROCESSED CORN), WHICH IS SIMMERED WITH STOCK UNTIL IT BECOMES SOFT AND CREAMY. HERE THE HOLY TRINITY OF ANY NEW ORLEANS GUMBO – SHRIMP, HOT TOMATO SAUCE AND CAJUN SMOKED TURKEY SAUSAGE – SPICE UP REGULAR OLD HOMINY GRITS VERY NICELY.

900 g/2 lbs. small-medium prawns/shrimp, peeled and deveined

60 g/4 tablespoons unsalted butter

6 small garlic cloves, crushed/minced

1 tablespoon canola oil, plus extra as needed

225 g/8 oz. Cajun-style smoked turkey or chicken sausage

1 tablespoon plain/all-purpose flour

1 white onion, chopped

½ green (bell) pepper, deseeded and chopped

1 celery stick, chopped

400-g/14-oz. can chopped tomatoes, well drained

3 teaspoons Cajun seasoning

375 ml/1½ cups chicken or vegetable stock

125 ml/½ cup double/heavy cream

150 g/1 cup uncooked quick grits/instant polenta

180 g/2 cups grated/shredded Cheddar cheese

salt and freshly ground black pepper

chilli flakes/hot red pepper flakes (optional)

spring onions/scallions, sliced, to garnish

SERVES 4

Fill a saucepan with 1 litre/4 cups water and place over low heat for the grits. You want to keep the water warmed so that you can start the grits quickly.

Arrange the prawns/shrimp in an even layer on a baking sheet covered with paper towels. Cover with paper towels and pat to remove as much moisture as possible. Set aside.

Heat 30 g/2 tablespoons of the butter in a large frying pan/skillet and sauté the garlic until just tender. Scrape out and set the butter and garlic aside in a small bowl.

In the same frying pan/skillet, add the canola oil. Over medium heat, sauté the sausage. Remove the sausage and set aside. To the same frying pan/skillet, add half of the prawns/shrimp and cook until barely pink. Remove and set aside with the sausage. Add the remaining prawns/shrimp and repeat.

Use the pan drippings and add enough extra canola oil to equal about 2 tablespoons, then add 15 g/1 tablespoon of the butter. Stir in the flour and cook, stirring, for about 3–4 minutes or until lightly browned.

Add the onion, (bell) pepper and celery, and cook, stirring, for about 3 minutes. Add the drained, chopped tomatoes and Cajun seasoning and cook for 3 minutes. Slowly add the stock and bring to the boil, then reduce the heat and simmer for 10 minutes.

While the sauce is simmering, bring the prepared water to the boil for the grits and stir in the cream. Slowly stir in the grits and cook for about 5 minutes, stirring regularly.

Add the prawns/shrimp and sausage back to the frying pan/skillet and heat through. To thicken the sauce, stir in the final 15 g/1 tablespoon of butter, taste and add salt and pepper as needed. Sprinkle with chilli flakes/hot red pepper flakes if desired.

To the grits, add the reserved cooked garlic and butter and the grated/shredded cheese. Stir until the cheese is incorporated and fully melted, then spoon the cheese grits into serving bowls, top with the shrimp mixture and garnish bowls with sliced spring onion/scallion.

OYSTER ROCKEFELLER HASH

170 g/6 oz. oysters

6 tablespoons extra virgin
olive oil

2 slices white sandwich
bread

¾ teaspoon anise seeds,
crushed with pestle in
a mortar

1 onion, chopped

1 fennel bulb, cored and
chopped

1 kg/2 lb. Maris Piper/Yukon
Gold potatoes, peeled and
cut into 1cm/½ inch
cubes

4 garlic cloves,
crushed/minced (about
2 teaspoons)

1–2 pinches cayenne
pepper

285 g/10 oz. frozen chopped
spinach, thawed and
squeezed dry

4 eggs, at room temperature

salt and freshly ground
black pepper

*25-cm/10-inch cast-iron
or non-stick frying
pan/skillet*

SERVES 4

OYSTER ROCKEFELLER IS A DISH WHOSE ORIGINS REACH BACK AS FAR AS 1899 AND WAS NAMED AFTER THE RICHEST MAN IN THE WORLD AT THE TIME, JOHN D. ROCKEFELLER. IN ESSENCE THE DISH IS MADE UP OF OYSTERS, BUTTER, BREADCRUMBS AND HERBS. ADD IT TO POTATOES FOR A HEARTY YET DECADENT BREAKFAST.

Wash and drain the oysters in a sieve/strainer set over a bowl. Set aside.

Heat 2 tablespoons of the oil in the cast iron or non-stick frying pan/skillet over medium heat. While the oil is heating, tear the bread into 6–8 pieces, then use a food processor to pulse the bread into crumbs. Continue pulsing until the crumbs are uniform with no large bits remaining. Transfer the breadcrumbs to the hot oil. Sauté, stirring occasionally, until the crumbs are golden brown and crispy. Transfer to a bowl and toss with ½ teaspoon salt, ¼ teaspoon black pepper, and the crushed anise seeds. Set aside.

Add 4 tablespoons olive oil to the now empty frying pan/skillet. Return the pan to the hob/burner on medium heat, and add the onion and fennel. Sauté, stirring occasionally, until the onions and fennel have softened and just started to brown, about 7-8 minutes.

While the onion and fennel are cooking, toss the potatoes with the oil, ½ teaspoon salt, and ¼ teaspoon pepper in a large bowl. Pan-fry the potatoes for about 5–7 minutes, until soft. Set aside.

Once the onion and fennel have started to brown, add the garlic, 1 teaspoon salt, ¼ teaspoon black pepper and the cayenne pepper. Stir to combine. Add the spinach, breaking it up as you add it.

Add the potatoes. Stir to combine, then press into a single layer. Cook for about 3 minutes (until the potatoes start to brown), then stir, and press into a single layer again and cook another 3 or so minutes.

Coarsely chop the oysters. Add half of them to the hash. Stir the hash again, and taste for seasoning. Adjust with salt, pepper, or cayenne as desired. Reduce the heat to medium low. Press the hash into a single layer a final time. Sprinkle the remaining chopped oysters evenly over the surface of the hash. Using the back of a large spoon, make 4 indents in the hash to cradle the eggs. Crack an egg into each indent and season the eggs with salt and pepper. Cover the frying pan/skillet and cook until the eggs are just set, about 5 minutes.

Divide the hash into shallow bowls, taking care not to break the yolks. Sprinkle each serving with a generous portion of the toasted breadcrumbs.

Trini Saltfish Buljol

225 g/7 oz. salt cod or
bacalao

200 ml/¾ cup milk

1 fresh bay leaf

1 slice of lemon

25 g/2 tablespoons butter

5–6 mixed peppercorns

1 teaspoon Dijon mustard

1 large onion, very finely
chopped

1 large tomato, diced

1 ripe pointed red sweet
(bell) pepper, deseeded
and diced, or ordinary red
sweet (bell) pepper

1 Trinidad Congo chilli/chile,
deseeded and finely
chopped

1 Hungarian Hot Wax
chilli/chile, deseeded and
finely chopped

½ teaspoon freshly ground
black pepper

3 tablespoons olive oil

a few Cos/Romaine lettuce
leaves

2 hard-boiled/hard-cooked
eggs, sliced

1 avocado, sliced

SERVES 2–4

A VERY HOT BREAKFAST OR BRUNCH, THIS IS A GREAT INTRODUCTION TO
CARIBBEAN FOOD AND TO THE MANY AND VARIED WAYS OF USING SALT
COD (SALTFISH TO WEST INDIANS AND BACALAO TO SPANIARDS!) IT
ALWAYS LOOKS LIKE SUCH AN UNPROMISING INGREDIENT BUT YOU CAN'T
HELP BUT BECOME A FAN WHEN IT HELPS DELIVER FLAVOURS LIKE THESE.
THIS RECIPE IS GREAT ON A LEISURELY SUNDAY MORNING BUT JUST AS
NICE FOR A LIGHT DINNER.

You will need to start preparing the salad the day before you serve it. Put the salt cod in a
bowl, cover with cold water and let soak for 24 hours in the fridge, changing the water
frequently.

The next day, drain the soaked cod and pat dry with paper towels. Put the cod in a large
frying pan/skillet and add the milk, bay leaf, lemon, butter and peppercorns. Cover with a lid
and poach gently for 20 minutes, or until the fish is soft. Remove from the poaching liquor
(reserving the liquor) and let cool.

Debone and flake the fish into a bowl.

Return the pan of poaching liquor to medium heat and cook, stirring regularly to prevent a
skin forming. Once the liquid has reduced by half, remove the bay leaf, lemon and
peppercorns and discard. Remove from the heat and stir in the mustard. Let cool for a while,
until thickened.

To the flaked fish, add the onion, tomato, sweet (bell) pepper, chillies/chiles, black pepper
and olive oil and mix well. Serve on the lettuce leaves and garnish with the eggs and avocado.
Serve with the thickened milk/mustard combination in a small bowl.

Tip: Trinidad Congo chillies/chiles are members of the Habanero family of chillies/chiles. They
are renowned for their pungency and wonderful fruity flavour and aroma. If you can't get hold
of these, any Habanero/Scotch Bonnet variety of chilli/chile will work perfectly in this recipe.
Hungarian Hot Wax chillies/chiles are mild peppers that add a delicious crunch and a modest
kick to any salad. If these are not available, substitute with half a yellow sweet (bell) pepper.

Nasi Goreng
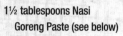

1½ tablespoons Nasi Goreng Paste (see below)

200 g/2 cups raw tiger prawns/jumbo shrimp

2 tablespoons vegetable oil

1 shallot, finely sliced

1 garlic clove, chopped

225 g/1½ cups cooked rice

2 teaspoons ketjap manis (sweet dark soy), plus extra to serve (optional)

1 teaspoon tomato purée/paste

1 teaspoon palm sugar/jaggery

2 small spring onions/scallions, chopped

1 egg

cucumber, tomatoes, sliced green chillies/chiles, to serve

Nasi goreng paste

25 g/¼ cup roasted salted peanuts

2 tablespoons vegetable oil

4 large garlic cloves roughly chopped

2 shallots, chopped

6 red chillies/chiles, roughly chopped

1 teaspoon blachan (dark shrimp paste)

1 teaspoon salt

SERVES 1

LIKE ANY OTHER MEAL, IF YOU ARE GOING TO HAVE BREAKFAST, WHY NOT DO IT PROPERLY? WITH THIS AIM IN MIND, THE IDEA OF A COOKED BREAKFAST IS ONE TO BE CELEBRATED – ESPECIALLY ONE THAT HAS A LITTLE HINT OF CHILLI/CHILE. CHILLI/CHILE GIVES THE BODY A WONDERFUL WAKE-UP CALL IN THE MORNING. NASI GORENG IS PRACTICALLY THE NATIONAL DISH IN INDONESIA. IT MAKES A FANTASTIC BREAKFAST OR BRINNER, AND IF YOU WANT A LITTLE MORE HEAT, JUST ADD A COUPLE OF FINELY SLICED CHILLIES/CHILES INTO THE WOK WHEN YOU'RE COOKING THE GARLIC.

To make the nasi goreng paste, put the peanuts in a food processor and briefly blitz them. Add the remaining ingredients and process until you have a thick paste – be sure to scrape down the sides of the bowl to ensure everything is evenly mixed. You can store this paste in an airtight container in the fridge, but it is better to make it fresh as required.

Put ½ tablespoon of the nasi goreng paste in a bowl. Add the prawns/shrimp and mix together to coat them – add a little oil if required to do this. Chill for 20 minutes in the fridge.

Heat the oil in a wok or frying pan/skillet over medium heat. Add the shallot and garlic and fry for 1 minute. Add the remaining nasi goreng spice paste and fry for a few minutes until the paste cooks and becomes aromatic. Tip in the rice and stir well to ensure it is evenly covered in the spicy paste. Add the ketjap manis, tomato purée/paste and palm sugar/jaggery and continue to fry, stirring constantly. Add the onions and prawns/shrimp and cook until the prawns/shrimp turn pink and are cooked through. Transfer to a serving plate. Keep warm.

Add a little more oil to the wok and heat over medium heat. Break the egg into the oil and fry until the edges begin to brown. Either spoon some of the oil over the egg to ensure even cooking, or flip the egg if you prefer.

To serve, place the egg on top of the nasi goreng and dress the plate with the slices of cucumber, tomato and chillies/chiles. Extra ketjap manis can be used as a condiment.

2 tablespoons cooking oil

1 teaspoon annatto seeds or saffron threads

1 onion, roughly chopped

450 g/1 lb. braising beef, beef tendons or rib, cubed

2 teaspoons chilli flakes/ hot red pepper flakes

1 teaspoon ground cumin

10 star anise

1 bay leaf

1 teaspoon paprika

½ teaspoon ground cloves

2 garlic cloves, sliced

2-cm/1-inch piece of fresh ginger, coarsely chopped

2 lemongrass stalks, outer layer removed, finely chopped

400 ml/1⅔ cups coconut water

100 ml/⅓ cup beef stock

2 carrots, roughly sliced

2 medium potatoes, cubed

1 teaspoon sugar

3 tablespoons fish sauce

1 teaspoon cornflour/ cornstarch

130 g/1 cup frozen peas

freshly ground black pepper

280 g/10 oz. thick rice vermicelli, cooked,

SERVES 4

BEEF STEW
with *star anise*

THE ULTIMATE COMFORT FOOD, BÒ KHO IS SPICY AND FRAGRANT ENOUGH TO AWAKEN THE SENSES AT THE START OF THE DAY IN VIETNAM, BUT IT IS ALSO PERFECT ENJOYED AS A COMFORTING EVENING MEAL. IT IS A THRIFTY DISH DESIGNED TO MAKE USE OF CHEAP CUTS OF BEEF AND WHICHEVER VEGETABLES YOU HAVE THAT NEED TO BE USED. OPTIONAL GARNISHES TO TRY ARE LIME WEDGES, BEANSPROUTS, THAI SWEET BASIL, GARDEN MINT AND CORIANDER/CILANTRO.

Heat the oil in a large saucepan over medium heat. Sauté the annatto seeds (or saffron) for a couple of minutes until the reddish colour is released. Pour the oil into a bowl and discard the seeds (it's okay to leave the saffron in).

In the same pan over low heat, gently fry the onion until softened. Turn the heat up to high and add the beef. Fry it, turning it often, until browned all over. You may need to do this in batches – if the meat is too cramped, it will stew rather than sear properly.

Add the chilli flakes/hot red pepper flakes, cumin, star anise, bay leaf, paprika, cloves, garlic, ginger and lemongrass and pour in the cider, stock and reserved red annatto oil. Stir well. Cover the pan with the lid and cook for about 15 minutes.

Add the carrots and potatoes and season with the sugar and fish sauce. Reduce the heat to low–medium and cook with the lid on for a further 30 minutes.

Put the cornflour/cornstarch and a few drops of water in a small bowl and stir to mix. Add it to the stew, along with the peas, and cook for 5–10 minutes, stirring occasionally, until the sauce has thickened slightly. The beef should be tender, but the cooking time may vary so braise it for longer if it is still tough. Season with more fish sauce or pepper, to taste, and remove the star anise. Serve with the vermicelli.

For the garnishes, squeeze the lime into the stew and serve any other garnishes on the side.

Fried Corn Tortillas
with *chilli tomato sauce & cheese*

vegetable oil, for frying

10 corn tortillas, cut into eighths

2 tomatoes

5 dried Chiles de Arbol (or other hot dried red chillies/chiles), seeded and stalks removed

1 teaspoon paprika

½ onion, finely chopped

2 eggs

a pinch of salt

100 g/1 cup grated/ shredded Cheddar cheese

refried black or pinto beans, to serve (optional)

SERVES 4

THIS IS A TRADITIONAL MEXICAN BREAKFAST DISH WHICH HAS ITS TWISTS AND VARIATIONS IN EVERY REGION IN MEXICO. IT IS A GREAT AND TASTY WAY TO MAKE USE OF LEFTOVER TORTILLAS AND SALSAS.

Pour some vegetable oil into a deep saucepan until it comes 2 cm/¾ inch up the side of the pan. Set over medium heat and leave until the oil is very hot but not smoking.

Carefully drop in the tortilla triangles, in batches of 10, and fry for about 30 seconds, turning the chips gently and often with tongs to prevent them from burning.

Using the tongs or a slotted spoon, remove the chips from the pan and allow to drain on paper towels. Repeat the process until all the chips have been fried. Reserve the oil.

Place 500 ml/2 cups water, the tomatoes and chillies/chiles in a saucepan and boil for 5 minutes.

Allow to cool for 10 minutes, then transfer all of it to a food processor with the paprika and whizz for 2 minutes or until smooth. Set aside.

Take 1 tablespoon of the reserved cooking oil and put in a large saucepan over medium heat.

Add the tortilla chips and onions to the pan, then add the eggs. Using a large spoon, very gently stir the mixture for 1 minute until the egg is cooked, but be careful not to break the fried tortilla chips.

Add the blended sauce, as well as the salt and cook for 3–5 minutes or until the sauce is heated through – do not overcook it otherwise the tortillas will turn soggy. They need to be mixed well with the sauce but still retain a little of their crunchiness.

Preheat the grill/broiler to medium.

Transfer the chilaquiles to an ovenproof dish and sprinkle the cheese over the top. Grill/broil for 1–2 minutes to melt the cheese. Serve with refried beans, if you like.

Chayote & Grapefruit Salad

3 tablespoons shelled
   pumpkin seeds

1 chayote (chow chow)

1 pink grapefruit or orange

1 small bunch of
   coriander/cilantro,
   chopped

1 tablespoon lime juice

2 tablespoons olive oil

¼ red onion, very thinly
   sliced

20 g/3 cups rocket/arugula

a pinch of paprika

a pinch of sea salt

SERVES 2

CHAYOTE (OR CHOW CHOW AS IT IS SOMETIMES KNOWN) IS A MEMBER OF THE GOURD FAMILY. IT HAS A MILD TASTE BUT THIS MEANS THAT IT HAPPILY ABSORBS AND TAKES ON THE FLAVOURS OF THE LIME, PAPRIKA AND SALT IN THIS MEXICAN SALAD. THE GOAL HERE IS TO COOK IT JUST ENOUGH TO SOFTEN IT BUT STILL LEAVE IT WITH A DELIGHTFUL CRUNCH.

Put the pumpkin seeds in a dry frying pan/skillet over low heat. Stir constantly for 7–10 minutes, taking care not to let them burn. Remove from the heat and set aside.

Put the whole chayote in a saucepan and cover with water. Bring to the boil, then simmer for 10 minutes. Drain and set aside to cool slightly.

When the chayote has cooled, cut it in half, remove the stone/pit and cut each half into thin wedges.

Peel the grapefruit, remove the bitter white pith and cut the flesh into neat segments.

To serve, mix all the ingredients together in a large bowl.

NOTE: chayote is a pale green, furrowed fruit, also known as a chow chow, christophene, mirliton or vegetable pear. In fact it is similar in shape to and slightly larger than a big pear, but its subtle flavour is closer to that of cucumber. It has featured in Mexican cuisine since the time of the Aztecs and Mayans and is now also popular in the USA and UK. Chayote can be eaten raw or cooked, when it should be prepared as you would a summer squash.

From the griddle

BUTTERMILK PANCAKES
with salmon & horseradish cream

170 g/1⅓ cups self-
raising/self-rising flour,
sifted

1 teaspoon baking powder

2 eggs, separated

200 ml/⅔ cup buttermilk

2 teaspoon
caster/granulated sugar

1 tablespoon finely
chopped/snipped chives,
plus extra for sprinkling

100 ml/⅓ cup milk

250 ml/1 cup crème fraîche

1 heaped tablespoon
creamed horseradish

1–2 tablespoons butter, for
frying

400 g/2½ cups smoked
salmon, to serve

1 lemon, sliced into wedges,
to serve

salt and freshly ground
black pepper

SERVES 4

BELLINI PANCAKES TOPPED WITH SMOKED SALMON MAKE FANTASTIC
CANAPÉS. FOR A MORE INDULGENT VERSION WHY NOT SERVE LARGE,
FLUFFY BUTTERMILK PANCAKES SEASONED WITH CHIVES AND TOPPED
WITH THICK SLICES OF SMOKED SALMON AND HORSERADISH CREAM?
THIS IS GREAT AS A BRUNCH DISH OR A LIGHT LUNCH OR SUPPER.

To make the pancake batter, put the flour, baking powder, egg yolks, buttermilk,
caster/granulated sugar and chives in a large mixing bowl and whisk together. Season well
with salt and pepper, then gradually add the milk until the batter is smooth and pourable.

In a separate bowl, whisk the egg whites to stiff peaks. Gently fold the whisked egg whites
into the batter mixture using a spatula. Cover and put in the refrigerator to rest for 30
minutes.

For the horseradish cream, whisk together the crème fraîche and horseradish in a mixing
bowl and season with salt and pepper.

When you are ready to serve, remove the batter mixture from the refrigerator and stir once.
Put a little butter in a large frying pan/skillet set over medium heat. Allow the butter to melt
and coat the base of the pan, then ladle small amounts of the rested batter into the pan,
leaving a little space between each. Cook until the underside of each pancake is golden
brown and a few bubbles start to appear on the top – this will take about 2–3 minutes.
Turn the pancake over using a spatula and cook on the other side until golden brown.

Serve the pancakes warm, topped with a generous spoon of the horseradish cream, slices of
smoked salmon and wedge of lemon to squeeze over the top. Sprinkle with extra
chopped/snipped chives and enjoy.

Beer & Bacon Pancakes

200 g/1½ cups smoked bacon lardons or diced pancetta

160 g/1¼ cups self-raising/self-rising flour, sifted

1 teaspoon baking powder

1 egg, separated

60 g/⅓ cup soft dark brown sugar

a pinch of salt

250 ml/1 cup beer

3 tablespoons melted butter, plus extra for frying

12 rashers/slices smoked streaky/fatty bacon, to serve (optional)

vegetable oil, for frying (optional)

maple syrup, to drizzle

SERVES 6

THESE PANCAKES ARE VERY MANLY! IN PLACE OF MILK, BEER IS USED TO BIND THE BATTER. IT GIVES THE PANCAKES A SAVOURY, MALTY FLAVOUR, AND WITH THE ADDITION OF SALTY BACON AND SWEET MAPLE SYRUP, THEY REALLY ARE THE PERFECT SWEET AND SAVOURY COMBINATION.

Begin by frying the bacon lardons in a dry frying pan/skillet – they will release sufficient oil as you cook them to prevent them sticking so you do not need to add any extra fat to the pan. Remove from the pan and put on a paper towel to remove any excess fat. Set aside while you prepare the batter.

To make the pancake batter, put the flour, baking powder, egg yolk, soft dark brown sugar, salt and beer in a large mixing bowl and whisk together. Add in the melted butter and cooked bacon lardons and whisk again. The batter should have a smooth, dropping consistency.

In a separate bowl, whisk the egg white to stiff peaks. Gently fold the whisked egg white into the batter mixture using a spatula. Cover and put in the refrigerator to rest for 30 minutes.

When you are ready to serve, remove your batter mixture from the refrigerator and stir gently. Put a little butter in a large frying pan/skillet set over medium heat. Allow the butter to melt and coat the base of the pan, then ladle small amounts of the rested batter into the pan, leaving a little space between each. Cook until the underside of each pancake is golden brown and a few bubbles start to appear on the top – this will take about 2–3 minutes. Turn the pancake over using a spatula and cook on the other side until golden brown. If you are serving with bacon rashers/slices, then gently fry these in a little vegetable oil until crisp in a separate pan while you work on the pancakes so that everything is hot when you are ready to serve.

Serve the pancakes with the streaky/fatty bacon and lashings of maple syrup.

Pulled Pork & Cheddar Hotcakes

520 g/4 cups plain/all-purpose flour

1 teaspoon salt

4 teaspoons baking powder

500 ml/2 cups milk

500 ml/2 cups buttermilk

2 eggs

300 g/2 cups leftover cooked pulled pork (see page 64) or cooked pork belly, as preferred

270 g/3 cups grated/shredded Cheddar cheese

a handful of freshly chopped dill (optional)

butter, for frying and serving

syrup, to serve

Serves 4

Pork and cheddar pancakes put a spin on the old ham and cheese sandwich. This fluffy pancake batter is sprinkled with roasted pork belly or leftover cooked pulled pork (see page 64), Cheddar and a little dill for extra flavour. Serve with or without the syrup – it's optional but certainly not essential.

Stir together the flour, salt and baking powder. Add the milk, buttermilk and eggs and stir well with an egg-beater or whisk until there are no lumps. Cover and let rest in the fridge for 30–60 minutes.

To make the pancakes, heat about ½ tablespoon of butter in a non-stick or cast-iron frying pan/skillet over medium-high heat. Add about 80 ml/⅓ cup of the batter and smooth out with ladle or spoon to make a circle.

Sprinkle with a few tablespoons of pork, about 20 g/¼ cup grated/shredded cheese and a sprinkle of dill, if using. Drizzle with a bit more batter over the top. When the batter forms large bubbles, flip the pancake over and continue cooking until cooked through.

Remove and keep warm while you cook the remaining pancakes. Use a little butter in the pan for every pancake, or as needed. Serve hot with butter and syrup.

Applesauce

4 green apples, peeled, cored and chopped

60 ml/¼ cup white sugar

½ teaspoon ground cinnamon

Breakfast sausages

15 g/1 tablespoon butter

1 sweet apple, peeled, cored and chopped

1 small white onion, finely chopped

1 teaspoon fennel seeds

700 g/1½ lbs. minced/ground chicken breast

1½ tablespoons freshly chopped sage

½ tablespoon soft light

1–2 teaspoons olive oil

salt and freshly ground black pepper

Pancakes

200 g/1½ cups plain/all-purpose flour

2 tablespoons white sugar

2 teaspoons baking powder

½ teaspoon bicarbonate of soda/baking soda

½ teaspoon salt

300–360 ml/1¼–1½ cups full-fat/whole milk

2 eggs, beaten

30 g/2 tablespoons butter, melted

pure maple syrup, to serve

SERVES 4

"CHICKS IN A BLANKET"
with *applesauce & maple syrup*

"PIGS IN A BLANKET" IS A SLANG TERM FOR PANCAKES WRAPPED AROUND BREAKFAST SAUSAGES. THEY ARE THE HOLY-GRAIL BRUNCH ITEM FOR THOSE WHO LIKE TO DIP THEIR SAUSAGE IN SYRUP. THESE "CHICKS" ARE NOT MADE WITH PORK SAUSAGE, BUT INSTEAD WITH CHICKEN-APPLE BREAKFAST SAUSAGES AND SERVED WITH A US-STYLE APPLESAUCE.

For the applesauce, combine the apples, sugar and cinnamon with 175 ml/¾ cup water in a saucepan or pot over medium heat. Cover and cook over medium heat for 15–20 minutes or until the apples are soft. Allow to cool, then mash with a fork or potato masher. Set aside until ready to serve.

For the chicken-apple breakfast sausages, heat a small non-stick frying pan/skillet over medium heat. Add the butter and melt. Add the apples and onion and season with a little salt, pepper and fennel seeds. Gently cook the mixture 5–7 minutes to soften. When cooked, remove from heat and set aside.

Heat a large non-stick frying pan/skillet over medium-high heat. Place the chicken in a bowl and season well with salt and pepper, add the sage and sugar and a few teaspoons of olive oil. Add the apple, onion and fennel seed mixture and use your hands to mix well. Using floured hands, divide the mixture and shape into twelve even-sized sausages.

Cook the sausages in the frying pan/skillet for 3–4 minutes, then flip and cook another 2–4 minutes, until cooked through. Remove from the pan and set aside.

For the pancakes, in a bowl, mix together all the dry ingredients and make a well in the centre. Start with 300 ml/1¼ cups milk, adding up to another 60 ml/¼ cup if necessary, as you mix it with the flour. Add the beaten eggs and melted butter, combining with a whisk until well-mixed but still a bit lumpy.

Heat a frying pan/skillet and add a teaspoonful or 2 of oil. When hot, pour in a ladleful of pancake mix at a time. When the pancake starts to bubble on top and is turning golden brown on the under-side, turn it and continue cooking until both sides are golden brown. Repeat the cooking process with the remaining batter until you have about 12 pancakes.

Keep the cooked pancakes covered with a clean dish towel, to keep them warm while you finish cooking the rest. Once all pancakes are cooked, wrap them around the sausages to form a roll with the sausages in the middle. Serve covered in maple syrup and alongside the homemade applesauce.

Squash & Goats' Cheese Pancakes

1 butternut squash, peeled and seeds removed (700 g/2½ lb), diced

2 tablespoons olive oil

1 teaspoon black onion seeds

a pinch of spiced sea salt or regular sea salt

4–5 curry leaves, crushed

1–2 garlic cloves, skins on

200 g/1⅔ cups self-raising/self-rising flour, sifted

2 teaspoons baking powder

1 egg

300 ml/1¼ cups milk

3 tablespoons melted butter, plus extra for greasing

125 g/1 cup soft goats' cheese

sour cream, to serve

a bunch of Greek basil leaves, to garnish

pumpkin seed oil, to drizzle

salt and freshly ground black pepper

an ovenproof roasting pan, greased

SERVES 4

PERFECT FOR LUNCH, THESE PANCAKES ARE TOPPED WITH SOUR CREAM OR CRÈME FRAÎCHE AND DRIZZLED WITH DELICIOUS PUMPKIN SEED OIL. USE A MILD, CREAMY GOATS' CHEESE SO THAT THE FLAVOUR IS NOT OVERPOWERING. HALEN MÔN SEA SALT (AVAILABLE ONLINE) WORKS WELL IN THIS RECIPE AS IT IS FRAGRANCED WITH CUMIN, NUTMEG, PAPRIKA, CLOVES AND CINNAMON AND GOES REALLY WELL WITH THE SPICED SQUASH.

Preheat the oven to 180°C (350°F) Gas 4.

Put the diced butternut squash in the prepared roasting pan. Drizzle with the olive oil and sprinkle over the onion seeds, salt and curry leaves. Stir so that the squash is well coated in the oil and spices, then add the garlic cloves to the pan. Roast in the preheated oven for 35–45 minutes until the squash is soft and starts to caramelize at the edges. Leave to cool completely.

To make the pancake batter, put the flour, baking powder, egg and milk in a large mixing bowl and whisk together. Season with salt and pepper. Add the melted butter and whisk again. The batter should have a smooth, dropping consistency. Add about two-thirds of the butternut squash to the batter and set aside.

Remove the skins from the garlic cloves and mash to a paste using a fork. Whisk into the batter then crumble in the goats' cheese. Mix together gently. Cover and put in the refrigerator to rest for 30 minutes.

Put a little butter in a large frying pan/skillet set over medium heat. Allow the butter to melt and coat the base of the pan, then ladle spoonfuls of the rested batter into the pan, leaving a little space between each.

Cook until the underside of each pancake is golden brown and a few bubbles start to appear on the top – this will take about 2–3 minutes. Turn the pancake over using a spatula and cook on the other side until golden brown.

Serve the pancakes topped with a spoonful of sour cream, a few sprigs of basil and the reserved butternut squash. Drizzle with pumpkin seed oil and sprinkle with freshly ground black pepper.

Courgette & Feta Griddle Cakes

150 g/heaped 1 cup self-raising/self-rising flour, sifted

2 eggs, separated

250 ml/1 cup milk

75 g/⅓ cup butter, melted and cooled, plus extra for frying

1 teaspoon baking powder

1 large courgette/zucchini, grated/shredded (about 200 g/2½ cups)

200 g/1½ cups feta cheese, crumbled

1 tablespoon freshly chopped mint

salt and freshly ground black pepper

MAKES 10

THESE PANCAKES ARE QUICK AND EASY TO PREPARE AND MAKE A GREAT SIDE TO SOUPS AS AN ALTERNATIVE TO BREAD. THE FETA CHEESE MELTS WHEN COOKED, GIVING THEM A LOVELY SOFT TEXTURE. YOU CAN MAKE THESE PANCAKES WITH RAW COURGETTE/ZUCCHINI, BUT IF YOU PREFER YOU CAN FRY THEM UNTIL SOFT IN A LITTLE OLIVE OIL BEFORE ADDING TO THE PANCAKE BATTER, MAKING SURE THAT YOU DRAIN THE COURGETTE/ZUCCHINI OF ITS COOKING JUICES AND COOL FIRST.

To make the pancake batter, put the flour, egg yolks, milk, melted butter and baking powder in a large mixing bowl and whisk together. Season well with salt and pepper and mix again until you have a smooth batter.

In a separate bowl, whisk the egg whites to stiff peaks. Gently fold the whisked egg whites into the batter mixture using a spatula. Cover and put in the refrigerator to rest for 30 minutes.

When you are ready to serve, remove the batter mixture from the refrigerator and stir gently. Add the grated/shredded courgette/zucchini to the batter with the feta cheese and mint.

Put a little butter in a large frying pan/skillet set over medium heat. Allow the butter to melt and coat the base of the pan, then ladle small amounts of the rested batter into the pan, leaving a little space between each. Cook until the underside of each pancake is golden brown and a few bubbles start to appear on the top – this will take about 2–3 minutes. Turn the pancake over using a spatula and cook on the other side until golden brown. It is important that they cook all the way through to ensure that the middles of your pancakes are not soggy.

Serve immediately.

Blueberry Cotton Candy Pancakes

200 g/1½ cups plain/all-purpose flour

1 tablespoon caster/granulated sugar

1 tablespoon brown sugar

1 teaspoon baking powder

½ teaspoon bicarbonate of soda/baking soda

½ teaspoon salt

2 eggs, at room temperature

250 ml/1 cup milk

235 g/1 cup sour cream or plain Greek yogurt

115 g/½ cup butter, melted

6 drops cotton candy flavouring

½ teaspoon pure vanilla extract

225 g/1½ cups fresh or frozen blueberries, plus extra to serve

maple syrup, to serve

Maple whipped cream

1½ tablespoons maple syrup

500 ml/2 cups single/light cream

SERVES 4

BLUEBERRY COTTON CANDY PANCAKES MIX A LITTLE BIT OF FAIRGROUND NOSTALGIA INTO BREAKFAST, SO THIS DISH IS PERFECT FOR BOTH A DREARY MONDAY MORNING AND A MIDNIGHT FEAST. THE TARTNESS OF THE BLUEBERRIES BALANCES OUT THE SWEET COTTON CANDY FLAVOUR TO MAKE A FUN SUPPER, DESSERT OR SNACK AT ANY TIME OF DAY.

Sift or whisk the dry ingredients (flour, sugars, baking powder, bicarbonate of soda/baking soda and salt) together in a large mixing bowl. In a separate large bowl, lightly whisk the eggs. Add the milk and the sour cream or Greek yogurt, half the melted butter, the cotton candy flavouring and the vanilla, whisking to incorporate.

Make a well in the dry ingredients and pour the egg mixture into it. Whisk the ingredients together until combined, then fold the blueberries into the batter.

Heat a large frying pan/skillet over medium heat and coat with some of the remaining melted butter. Pour a small ladleful of the batter into the centre of the pan. When bubbles begin to form and "pop" on the pancake's surface, after about 1 minute, and the outer edge looks done, flip it over and cook briefly for about 30 seconds on the other side. Transfer to a warm plate until ready to serve. Repeat until the batter is used up, adding a little butter to the pan each time before adding the batter.

To make the maple whipped cream, add the cream and the maple syrup to a mixing bowl and whisk with a hand-mixer or a free standing-mixer until the whipped cream forms soft peaks.

Serve with extra maple syrup and fresh blueberries.

Granola Pancakes
with salty honey sauce

160 g/1¼ cups self-raising/rising flour, sifted

1 teaspoon baking powder

1 egg, separated

1 tablespoon orange blossom honey

a pinch of salt

250 ml/1 cup milk

3 tablespoons melted butter, plus extra for frying

120–150 g/1½–2 cups crunchy granola

Salty honey sauce

60 g/4 tablespoons butter

3½ tablespoons clear honey

½ teaspoon salt

120 ml/½ cup double/heavy cream

MAKES 6

THESE ARE FANTASTIC BREAKFAST PANCAKES, BUT JUST AS DELICIOUS IN THE EVENING WHEN YOU FANCY A SWEET BITE. THEY HAVE A CRUNCHY, OATY TOP AND ARE SERVED WITH A DELICIOUS, BUTTERY, HONEY SAUCE. YOU CAN ALSO ADD (DARK) RAISINS, SULTANAS/LIGHT RAISINS, DRIED BERRIES AND CHERRIES TO THE BATTER FOR AN EXTRA FRUITY TANG.

To make the pancake batter, put the flour, baking powder, egg yolk, honey, salt and milk in a large mixing bowl and whisk together. Add in the melted butter and whisk again. The batter should have a smooth, dropping consistency.

In a separate bowl, whisk the egg white to stiff peaks. Gently fold the whisked egg white into the batter mixture using a spatula. Cover and put in the refrigerator to rest for 30 minutes.

For the sauce, heat the butter and honey in a small saucepan or pot until the butter has melted. Then add the salt and whisk in the cream over the heat. Keep the pan on the heat but turn it down to low to keep the sauce warm until you are ready to serve.

When you are ready to serve, remove your batter mixture from the refrigerator and stir once. Put a little butter in a large frying pan/skillet set over medium heat. Allow the butter to melt and coat the base of the pan, then ladle the batter into the pan and sprinkle a little granola on top of the pancake. Cook until the underside of the pancake is golden brown and a few bubbles start to appear on the top – this will take about 2–3 minutes. Turn the pancake over using a spatula and cook on the other side until golden brown. Keep the pancake warm while you cook the remaining batter, adding a little more butter to the pan each time if necessary.

Serve the pancakes with the warm honey sauce poured over the top.

CHERRY & RICOTTA BLINTZES *with* *sour cherry soup*

BLINTZES ARE ESSENTIALLY A PANCAKE WITHOUT ANY RAISING AGENT, SIMILAR TO A CRÊPE. POPULAR IN RUSSIAN AND JEWISH CULTURE, THEY ARE SERVED USUALLY AT POTLUCKS OR FOR DESSERT. THIS RECIPE USES A HOMEMADE CHERRY SAUCE AND IS ACCOMPANIED BY A COLD SOUR CHERRY SOUP, TO MAKE A WONDERFUL BREAKFAST OR DESSERT.

375 ml/1½ cups semi-skimmed/skim milk

3 eggs

30 g/2 tablespoons butter, melted

90 g/⅔ cup plain/all-purpose flour

½ teaspoon salt

Cheese filling

225 g/1 cup ricotta cheese

85 g/3 oz. cream cheese, softened

50 g/¼ cup sugar

½ teaspoon vanilla extract

Cherry sauce

450 g/1 lb. fresh or frozen pitted cherries

50 g/¼ cup sugar

1 tablespoon cornflour/cornstarch

SERVES 4

In a small bowl, combine the milk, eggs and butter. Set aside. In another small or medium bowl, combine the flour and salt together by whisking. Add the flour and salt mixture into the milk mixture and combine. Cover and refrigerate for 2 hours.

Heat a lightly greased 20 cm/8 inch non-stick frying pan/skillet and pour 2 tablespoons of the batter into the centre of the frying pan/skillet. Lift and tilt pan to coat the bottom evenly. Cook until the top appears dry. Using a small off-set spatula, daintily turn it over and cook for 15–20 seconds longer. Remove to a wire rack to cool. Repeat with the remaining batter.

Stack the cooled crêpes with waxed paper or paper towels in between, then wrap in foil and refrigerate.

Preheat the oven to 180°C (350°F) Gas 4.

In a blender or food processor, process the ricotta until smooth. Transfer to a small bowl. Add the cream cheese and beat until smooth. Beat in the sugar and vanilla.

Spread about 1 rounded tablespoonful onto each crêpe. Fold the opposite sides of the crêpe over the filling, forming a little bundle. Place seam-side down in the greased baking pan. Repeat with the remaining crêpes. Bake, uncovered, in the preheated oven for 10 minutes or until heated through.

Meanwhile, for the sauce, in a large saucepan, bring the cherries, sugar and 160 ml/⅔ cup water to the boil over medium heat. Reduce the heat, cover and simmer for 5 minutes or until heated through.

Combine the cornflour/cornstarch with 1 tablespoon water until it forms a smooth paste. Stir the cornflour/cornstarch mixture into the cherry mixture. Bring to the boil and cook for 2 minutes (or until desired consistency is reached), stirring constantly.

Serve slightly warm with hot blintzes and Cold Cherry Soup (see recipe **left**).

Sour cherry soup

340 g/¾ lb. sweet, dark
   cherries, stoned/pitted

50 g/¼ cup sugar

60 ml/¼ cup good red wine
   (ideally a jammy Pinot
   Noir)

½ teaspoon salt

1 tablespoon finely grated
   lemon zest

100 g/½ cup plain
   Greek-style/strained
   yogurt

SERVES 4

To make the sour cherry soup, place the cherries in a bowl and the stones/pits in a large saucepan or soup pot. Add 600 ml/2½ cups water to the saucepan or soup pot and bring to a boil. Reduce the heat and simmer for 5 minutes.

With a skimmer, remove the stones/pits from the water. Add the sugar, red wine, salt and lemon zest, and bring back to a boil over medium-high heat. Boil for 3 minutes, then add the stoned/pitted cherries, reserving a few for garnishing. Turn the heat to low, cover and simmer 5 minutes. Remove from the heat and set aside.

Put the yogurt in a large bowl and slowly whisk in 125 ml/½ cup of the liquid from the soup. Whisk until the mixture is smooth. Slowly add the rest of the soup, and whisk or stir until smooth.

Allow the soup to cool, stirring from time to time, then refrigerate until cold. When ready to serve, remove from the refrigerator and give the soup a mix to recombine ingredients.

Serve in bowls and garnish with the reserved chopped, stoned/pitted cherries.

Oreo Pancakes
with chocolate fudge sauce

160 g/1¼ cups self-
raising/self-rising flour,
sifted

1 teaspoon baking powder

1 egg, separated

1 teaspoon pure vanilla
extract/vanilla bean paste

2 tablespoons
caster/granulated sugar

a pinch of salt

250 ml/1 cup milk

2 tablespoons melted butter,
plus extra for frying

9 Oreo cookies or similar,
broken into pieces

Chocolate fudge sauce.

30 g/⅓ cup cocoa powder,
sifted

1 teaspoon cold water

150 ml/⅔ cup double/
heavy cream

100 g/⅓ cup milk chocolate,
chopped

1 tablespoon golden
syrup/light corn syrup

1 tablespoon butter

a pinch of salt

1 teaspoon pure vanilla
extract/vanilla bean paste

MAKES 12

THE OREO PIECES SOFTEN WHEN COOKED AND CREATE DELICIOUSLY CHOCOLATEY BURSTS WITHIN THE PANCAKE. SERVED WITH A WICKEDLY SWEET CHOCOLATE SAUCE, THESE ARE DEFINITELY PANCAKES FOR A SPECIAL TREAT RATHER THAN EVERY DAY.

To make the pancake batter, put the flour, baking powder, egg yolk, vanilla extract/vanilla bean paste, caster/granulated sugar, salt and milk in a large mixing bowl and whisk together. Add in the melted butter and whisk again. The batter should have a smooth, dropping consistency.

In a separate bowl, whisk the egg white to stiff peaks. Gently fold the whisked egg white into the batter mixture using a spatula. Cover and put in the refrigerator to rest for 30 minutes.

For the chocolate fudge sauce, mix the cocoa powder with a little cold water until you have smooth paste. Put the cream, chocolate, cocoa paste, golden syrup/light corn syrup, butter, salt and vanilla extract in a saucepan or pot set over medium heat and simmer until the chocolate has melted and you have a smooth, glossy sauce. Keep the pan on the heat but turn it down to low to keep the sauce warm until you are ready to serve.

When you are ready to serve, remove your batter mixture from the refrigerator and stir once. Put a little butter in a large frying pan/skillet set over medium heat. Allow the butter to melt and coat the base of the pan, then ladle small amounts of the batter into the pan. Sprinkle some of the Oreo cookies into the batter and cook until the batter is just set then turn over and cook for a further 2–3 minutes. Once cooked, keep the pancakes warm while you cook the remaining batter in the same way, adding a little butter to the pan each time, if required.

Serve the pancakes in a stack with the hot chocolate fudge sauce poured over the top.

peanut butter & jelly
FRENCH TOAST

4 large thick slices of
brioche or white bread

120 g/1 cup honey roasted
peanuts

4 eggs

120 ml/scant ½ cup
double/heavy cream

1 tablespoon
caster/granulated sugar

a pinch of salt

1–2 tablespoons butter, for
greasing

icing/confectioners' sugar
for dusting

Filling,

3 tablespoons crunchy
peanut butter

3 tablespoons fruit jam/jelly
(flavour of your choosing)

SERVES 4

PEANUT BUTTER AND JELLY IS A CLASSIC AMERICAN COMBINATION. THOSE OF YOU UNFAMILIAR WITH IT MAY FIND THE THOUGHT OF THIS A LITTLE STRANGE, BUT THE SWEET AND SALTY COMBINATION IS DELICIOUS AND CERTAINLY NOT AS PECULIAR AS IT SOUNDS. THESE FRENCH TOASTS ARE COATED IN SWEET HONEY-ROASTED PEANUTS, BUT IF YOU LIKE SALTY FLAVOURS YOU COULD REPLACE THEM WITH CRUSHED SALTED PEANUTS INSTEAD.

Using a sharp knife, cut a pocket in the top of each brioche slice to create a large cavity. Take care not to cut all the way through as it is this cavity which will hold your filling. Carefully spread some peanut butter and jam/jelly inside each pocket using a knife, then press the opening down to close the pocket.

Put the peanuts in a food processor and pulse to a fine crumb, then tip onto a large plate and set aside.

Whisk together the eggs, cream, caster/granulated sugar and salt in a mixing bowl, transfer to a shallow dish and set aside. Melt the butter in a large frying pan/skillet set over medium heat until the butter begins to foam. Soak each filled slice in the egg mixture on one side for a few seconds, then turn over and soak the other side. The slices should be fully coated in egg, but not too soggy – it is best to soak one slice at a time. Carefully move the slices to the peanut plate and coat in fine crumbs on both sides. Put each slice straight in the pan before soaking and cooking the next slice.

Cook for a few minutes on each side until the slices are golden brown, but taking care that the nuts do not burn. Keep the cooked toast warm while you cook the remaining slices in the same way, adding a little butter to the pan each time, if required.

Serve the toasts immediately, dusted with icing/confectioners' sugar.

The
Pastry basket

BUTTERSCOTCH-BACON BRITTLE CINNAMON ROLLS

IT SEEMS THAT A FEW YEARS AGO, THE BAKING WORLD WAS FILLED WITH THE MAPLE-BACON FAD. MOST OF US THOUGHT IT WAS INDEED A FAD AND WOULD SOON GO AWAY, BUT HERE IT SITS STILL. ALTHOUGH MAPLE-BACON CINNAMON ROLLS HAVE BEEN DONE BEFORE, THEY HAVE YET TO BE DONE IN THIS MANNER SO DO GIVE MY RECIPE A TRY... DELICIOUS SERVED ALONGSIDE A COFFEE GRANITA (SEE PAGE 147).

Brittle,

450 g/1 lb. cooked bacon, finely chopped

115 g/½ cup butter

100 g/½ cup caster/granulated sugar

225 g/1 cup butterscotch chips

Cinnamon rolls,

7-g/¼-oz. packet active dried yeast

250 ml/1 cup warm milk

100 g/½ cup white sugar

75 g/⅓ cup butter

1 teaspoon salt

2 eggs

500 g/4 cups plain/all-purpose flour

Filling,

180 g/1 cup packed brown sugar

2½ tablespoons ground cinnamon

75 g/⅓ cup soft butter

Icing,

115 g/8 tablespoons butter

200 g/1½ cups icing/confectioners' sugar

75 g/¼ cup cream cheese

½ teaspoon vanilla extract

a pinch of salt

a baking sheet lined with greased parchment paper

a large baking pan, lightly greased

MAKES 6–8

Preheat the oven to 200°C (400°F) Gas 6.

For the butterscotch-bacon brittle, spread the crushed bacon out on the lined baking sheet. In a medium saucepan, bring the butter and sugar to a boil, stirring and watching constantly as soon as you notice the sugar melting. Boil for about 3 minutes, then carefully pour the toffee mixture evenly over the bacon. Bake the toffee-covered bacon for about 4–5 minutes in the preheated oven. Remove from the oven. While the toffee is still really hot, sprinkle the butterscotch chips over the top to let them melt onto the toffee. Let the toffee cool completely before breaking the bacon into pieces. Set aside.

To make the cinnamon rolls, in a large bowl, dissolve the yeast in the warm milk. Add the sugar, butter, salt, eggs and flour, and mix well to combine.

Turn the dough out onto a lightly floured surface and knead for 5–10 minutes. Bring it together into a large ball, then put the dough in a bowl, cover and let rise in a warm place about 1 hour or until the dough has doubled in size.

Roll the dough out on a lightly floured surface, until it is approximately 54 x 40 cm/21 x 16 inches and 1 cm/⅓ inch thick.

Preheat the oven to 200°C (400°F) Gas 6.

To make filling, combine the brown sugar and cinnamon in a bowl. Add the butterscotch-bacon brittle. Spread the softened butter over the surface of the dough, then sprinkle the filling mixture evenly over the surface. Working carefully, from the long edge, roll the dough down to the bottom edge. Cut the dough into 4.5-cm/1¾-inch slices.

Place the slices in the prepared baking pan and bake in the preheated oven for 10–12 minutes or until light golden brown. Let cool in the pan.

Combine all the icing ingredients in a large bowl and beat on high speed with an electric mixer until thoroughly combined. Spread the cooled rolls generously with the icing. Serve.

BEIGNETS

2¼ teaspoons active dry yeast

375 ml/1½ cups warm water (45°C/110°F)

100 g/½ cup caster/granulated sugar

1 teaspoon salt

2 eggs

250 g/1 cup evaporated milk

900 g/7 cups plain/all-purpose flour

60 g/¼ cup shortening

1 litre/4 cups vegetable oil, for deep-frying

35 g/¼ cup icing/confectioners' sugar

MAKES 12

THESE NEW ORLEANS PILLOWS OF HEAVEN ARE AS GOOD AS IT GETS WHEN IT COMES TO DOUGHNUTS. SERVE WITH CHICORY COFFEE, DIP IN BUTTER OR GRATED PARMESAN OR JUST EAT PLAIN.

In a large bowl, dissolve yeast in the warm water. Add the sugar, salt, eggs and evaporated milk and blend well.

Mix in 500 g/4 cups of the flour and beat until smooth. Add the shortening and then the remaining flour. Cover and chill for up to 24 hours.

Roll out the dough to 3 mm/⅛ inch thick. Cut into 6-cm/2½-inch squares.

Heat the oil for deep-frying to 180°C (360°F).

Fry the beignets in the hot oil in batches until they rise to the surface. (If they do not pop up, the oil is not hot enough.) Remove with a slotted spoon and drain on paper towels.

Shake icing/confectioners' sugar on the hot beignets and serve warm.

Dough

Dough

250 ml/1 cup full-fat/whole milk

115 g/½ cup butter

100 g/½ cup caster/granulated sugar

2 x 7-g/¼-oz. packets active yeast, dissolved in 60 ml/¼ cup warm water

1 egg, beaten

½ teaspoon salt

1 teaspoon ground cardamom

about 520 g/4 cups plain/all-purpose flour

Filling

30 g/2 tablespoons butter, melted

50 g/¼ cup brown sugar, packed

1 tablespoon caster/granulated sugar

2 teaspoons ground cinnamon

140 g/1 cup sultanas/golden raisins (optional)

40 g/½ cup flaked/slivered almonds (optional)

75 g/¼ cup almond paste (optional)

Egg glaze

2 egg yolks

2 tablespoons any cream

Sugar glaze

140 g/1 cup icing/confectioners' sugar

a baking sheet, greased

MAKES 2 CAKES

CARDAMOM CAKE

THIS RECIPE IS A SWEDISH COFFEE BREAD, WHICH IS SERVED AS A HOLIDAY TRADITION DURING THE CHRISTMAS SEASON. HOWEVER, IT CAN BE ENJOYED YEAR ROUND.

Put the milk into a small saucepan and heat over medium heat until steaming but not boiling. Remove from the heat. Stir in the butter and sugar until the butter has melted and the sugar has dissolved. Pour into a mixing bowl and stir in the yeast mixture and egg.

Mix in the salt and cardamom, then slowly add in half of the flour. Gradually add more flour until a soft dough starts to form a ball and pull away from the sides of the bowl – you may not need all of the flour. Turn out onto a floured surface and knead the dough for 7–10 minutes until smooth. Place the dough in an oiled bowl, covered with a clean dish towel or with clingfilm/plastic wrap. Let rise for 1 hour or until the dough has doubled in size.

Press the dough down to deflate it a bit. Divide the dough into two equal parts. Take one half (saving the other for wreath number two) and use your fingers to spread it into a 20 x 40-cm/8 x 16-inch rectangle on a lightly floured surface. If you are having difficulty getting the dough to keep its shape, just let it sit for 5 minutes before trying again. Like pizza dough, the dough needs time to relax while you are forming it.

Brush the dough with the melted butter, leaving at least 1 cm/½ inch border on the edges so the dough will stick together when rolled. Mix together the brown and white sugar and the cinnamon, and sprinkle the dough with half of the mixture (saving the other half for the second batch of dough). Sprinkle on more fillings, as you like, such as sultanas/golden raisins, flaked/slivered almonds and almond paste.

Carefully roll the dough up lengthways, with the seam on the bottom. Transfer to the greased baking sheet. Form a circle with the dough, connecting the ends together. Using kitchen scissors, cut most of the way through the dough, cutting on a slant. Work your way around the dough circle. Repeat with the rest of the dough and filling ingredients to form a second wreath. Cover lightly with clingfilm/plastic wrap and let rise in a warm place for about 40–60 minutes; the dough should again puff up in size.

Preheat the oven to 175°C (350°F) Gas 4.

For the egg glaze, whisk together the egg yolks and cream. Use a pastry brush to brush the glaze over the dough. Bake in the preheated oven for 25–30 minutes. After the first 15 minutes of baking, if the top is getting well browned, cover it loosely with some foil.

Remove from oven and let cool completely. For the sugar glaze, whisk together the icing/confectioners' sugar with about 1 tablespoon water. Drizzle the glaze in a back-and-forth motion over the pastry. Let the glaze set before serving.

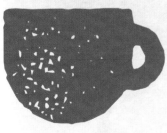

RASPBERRY COFFEE CAKE

375 ml/1½ cups lukewarm milk

2 x 7 g/¼ oz. packages active dried yeast

520 g/4 cups plain/all-purpose flour, plus extra as needed

100 g/½ cup caster/granulated sugar

2 teaspoons salt

225 g/1 cup cold unsalted butter, cut into 2.5 cm/ 1 inch pieces

4 egg yolks

290 g/1 cup raspberry jam/jelly

1 egg white, for brushing (optional)

Vanilla glaze

200 g/1½ cups icing/confectioners' sugar

½ teaspoon salt

1 teaspoon pure vanilla extract

about 4 tablespoons milk

23 x 30-cm/9 x 12-inch cake pan, greased

MAKES 2 CAKES

THIS COFFEE CAKE IS DELICIOUS AS A BREAKFAST TREAT, MID-AFTERNOON SNACK OR EVENING DESSERT. THIS YEASTED COFFEE CAKE IS BAKED WITH JAM IN BETWEEN FIVE STRIPS OF DOUGH AND THEN COVERED WITH A VANILLA GLAZE. IT PAIRS PERFECTLY WITH A GLASS OF MILK – THERE ISN'T A BETTER WAY TO START OR END THE DAY.

Preheat the oven to 175°C (350°F) Gas 4.

Put the warm milk and yeast in a bowl and stir, then set aside for 10 minutes until frothing.

Meanwhile, combine the flour, sugar and salt in a mixing bowl. Add the butter and blend it into the flour mixture with a large fork or pastry cutter, until you have pea-sized crumbs. Make a well in the middle of the mixture, add the yeast and milk and stir to combine. Mix in the egg yolks.

Dust the work surface with flour and turn out the cake mixture. With flour-dusted hands, form a sticky dough, slowly incorporating a little more flour as needed. Knead the dough until smooth and elastic, then divide the dough in half. (You can either make two coffee cakes now or freeze one half.)

Roll one portion of the dough into five long strips that are the length of your cake pan. Line them next to each other and press them together to combine them. There should be little concaved grooves in the dough from where they are joined; this is where you add your jam.

Take spoonfuls of the jam and gently fill the small, concaved spaces between the dough strips. Brush the dough with egg white (optional). Bake in the preheated oven for 30–40 minutes. Stick a cocktail stick/toothpick in the dough to test the bake (it should come out clean).

For the vanilla glaze, combine all the ingredients in a bowl and mix until the desired consistency is reached, adding extra milk if needed – it should be runny, yet still slightly firm. When the desired consistency is reached, pour the glaze over the cake and allow to set before serving.

CARROT CAKE SCONES

260 g/2 cups plain/all-purpose flour

1 tablespoon baking powder

50 g/¼ cup soft light brown sugar

1 teaspoon salt

1 teaspoon ground cinnamon

¼ teaspoon freshly ground nutmeg

¼ teaspoon ground ginger

a pinch of ground cardamon

a pinch of ground all-spice

a pinch of ground cloves

115 g/½ cup unsalted butter, cold and cubed

135 g/1 cup grated/shredded carrots

70 g/½ cup raisins

180 ml/¾ cup double/heavy cream, plus 60 ml/¼ cup for brushing

Cream cheese glaze,

60g/4 tablespoons unsalted butter, softened

55 g/¼ cup cream cheese, softened

280 g/2 cups icing/confectioners' sugar

a pinch of salt

1 teaspoon vanilla extract

1-4 teaspoons milk

50 g/½ cup pecan pieces

a 10-cm/4-inch round cookie cutter

a baking sheet, lined with baking parchment

MAKES 12

CARROT CAKE SCONES ARE A GREAT WAY TO GET IN A DOSE OF CARROT CAKE WITHOUT THE GUILT OF INDULGING IN A PIECE OF CAKE FOR BREAKFAST, ALTHOUGH THESE SCONES ARE JUST AS GOOD. THEY ARE SOFT, CRISP AND SPICY. GLAZE THEM OR LEAVE THEM PLAIN AND SPREAD WITH CREAM CHEESE WHILE THEY ARE STILL WARM FROM THE OVEN.

Preheat the oven to 175°C (350°F) Gas 4.

In a large bowl, combine the flour, baking powder, brown sugar, salt and spices. Add the cold diced butter and, using your fingertips, rub the butter into the flour mixture until it resembles coarse crumbs the size of peas. Stir in the carrots and raisins. Pour the 175 ml/¾ cup double/heavy cream and fold with a rubber spatula until the dough comes together.

Turn out onto a lightly floured work surface and knead a few times. Roll out into a large circle about 2 cm/¾ inch thick. Using the cutter, stamp out scones and place them on the prepared baking sheet. Gather the scraps and gently reroll. Cut out once again. Brush the scones with the extra cream.

Bake in the preheated oven for 18-20 minutes or until golden brown. Remove from oven and transfer to a wire rack to cool completely.

To make the glaze, mix together all of the ingredients, except for the pecans, in a large bowl. Add as much milk as needed to get a pourable consistency, but not too thin. Transfer to a disposable piping/pastry bag and snip off the tip. Drizzle the glaze over the cooled scones. Sprinkle with chopped pecans and allow to set for a few minutes before serving.

Leftovers can be stored at room temperature, well wrapped, for up to 2 days or in the fridge for up to 4 days. They can also be frozen.

JAM or CUSTARD BISMARKS

BISMARKS ARE SOFT FILLED DOUGHNUTS. THIS RECIPE MAKES THE PERFECT FLAKY DOUGHNUT TO FILL WITH JAM/JELLY OR CUSTARD.

- 7-g/¼-oz. packet active dry yeast
- 125 ml/½ cup lukewarm semi-skimmed milk, plus extra if needed
- 1 tablespoon caster/granulated sugar
- 260 g/2 cups flour, plus extra if needed
- ½ teaspoon salt
- 1 egg, beaten
- 15 g/1 tablespoon butter, melted and cooled
- vegetable oil, for deep-frying
- icing/confectioners' sugar, for dusting

Strawberry jam/jelly

- 900 g/2 lb. strawberries, hulled
- 800 g/4 cups caster/granulated sugar
- 60 ml/¼ cup freshly squeezed lemon juice

Vanilla custard

- 500 ml/2 cups milk
- 115 g/generous ½ cup caster/granulated sugar
- 2 egg yolks
- 1 egg, lightly beaten
- 25 g/¼ cup cornstarch
- 30 g/2 tablespoons butter
- 1 teaspoon pure vanilla extract

- a 7.5-cm/3-inch round cookie cutter, lightly floured
- 2 baking sheets, lightly floured

MAKES 10–12

In a small bowl, mix the yeast with the milk and sugar. Let sit for about 10 minutes, until foamy. In the bowl of a stand mixer fitted with the dough hook, combine the flour and salt. Add the yeast mixture. Add the egg and butter. Mix the ingredients into a soft, but not sticky, dough. (Add a little extra milk or extra flour, 1 tablespoon at a time, if needed). Knead the dough until smooth and elastic. Transfer the dough to a lightly oiled bowl, cover, and let rise until doubled in size, about 2 hours.

Knock back/punch down the dough. Turn it out onto a lightly floured surface and knead for a few seconds. With a lightly floured rolling pin, gradually roll out the dough to about 13 mm/½ inch thick. Cut out rounds with the cookie cutter, re-rolling scraps as you go. Place the doughnuts on the prepared baking sheets, spacing them apart, and cover lightly with a dry dish towel. Let rise in a warm spot until doubled in size, about 20 minutes.

Using a deep-fryer (or a heavy-bottomed saucepan or pot filled with 7.5-cm/3-inches of vegetable oil), heat the oil 160°C (325°F). Fry the doughnuts, a few at a time, until golden and puffed, about 4–5 minutes, turning frequently using a slotted spoon. Lift the doughnuts from the oil and place onto a cooling rack. Once cooled, fill a disposable piping/pastry bag with jam/jelly or custard and snip off the end. Insert the tip into the end of each doughnut and pipe approximately 1–2 teaspoons filling into them. Dust with sugar and eat the same day.

Strawberry Jam/Jelly Filling

Crush the strawberries in batches in a wide-rimmed bowl until you have 1 litre/4 cups of mashed berry. In a heavy-bottomed saucepan, mix together the strawberries, sugar and lemon juice. Stir over low heat until the sugar is dissolved. Increase heat to high, and bring the mixture to a full rolling boil. Boil, stirring often, until the mixture reaches 105°C (220°F) on a sugar thermometer. Refrigerate until using.

Vanilla Custard Filling

Stir together the milk and 50 g/¼ cup of the sugar in a large saucepan. Bring to a boil over medium heat. In a medium bowl, whisk together the egg yolks and beaten egg. Stir together the remaining sugar and cornflour/cornstarch, then stir them into the egg until smooth. When the milk comes to the boil, drizzle it into the bowl in a thin stream while mixing. Return the mixture to the saucepan, and slowly bring to a boil, stirring constantly. When the mixture comes to the boil and thickens, remove it from the heat. Stir in the butter and vanilla, mixing until the butter is completely blended in. Pour into a container and put a piece of clingfilm/plastic wrap directly on the surface to prevent a skin from forming. Chill well before using.

Habanero Marmalade

THIS FIERY MARMALADE CAN BE USED TO REALLY WAKE UP YOUR BREAKFAST OR SUPPER TOAST. IT IS HOT AND FRESH AND ZESTY ALL AT THE SAME TIME. IT ALSO MAKES AN UNUSUAL BUT WELCOME ADDITION TO ANY CHEESE BOARD.

750 g/1½ lbs. (about 2) slightly under-ripe grapefruits

500 g/1 lb. (about 3) slightly under-ripe limes

about 1.8 litres/2 quarts water

100 g/3½ oz. Habanero chillies/chiles, deseeded

2.5 kg/5½ lbs. granulated sugar

100 ml/⅓ cup freshly squeezed lemon juice

a piece of muslin/cheesecloth

kitchen twine

several jam jars, sterilized

MAKES ABOUT 3.5 KG/7½ LBS.

Peel the grapefruits and cut the peel into thick shreds. Do the same with the limes (if they're too difficult to peel, dice the whole lime as finely as possible and remove and set aside the seeds). Remove and set aside the seeds from the grapefruit. Squeeze the juice into a bowl and roughly chop the remaining pulp. Put the lime and grapefruit pulp, juice and peel in a large saucepan with the water. Put all the seeds in a piece of muslin/cheesecloth and tie with kitchen twine. Add to the pan. Bring to the boil, reduce the heat and gently simmer, uncovered, for 1½–1¾ hours. Remove the bag and squeeze any juice into the pan.

To a small bowl, add 150 ml/⅔ cup of the cooking liquid and the chillies/chiles. Blend to a smooth purée. Transfer back to the pan and stir. Add the sugar and lemon juice. Bring back to the boil and boil hard for 15–20 minutes. To see if the marmalade has reached setting point, drip a little onto a plate and chill. If it forms a skin, it is ready. If not, return to the heat and test again in 10 minutes.

Refrigerate and use within 1 month or for a longer life seal in sterilized jars using your preferred method.

GRAPE JELLY & LEMON CURD

Grape jelly

1.35 kg/3 lb. ripe Concord grapes, picked off of their stems

600 g/3 cups sugar

MAKES 1.25 LITRES/5 CUPS

Lemon curd

4 egg yolks

100 g/½ cup granulated sugar

finely grated zest of 5–6 lemons, depending on their size

80 ml/⅓ cup freshly squeezed lemon juice (from 3-4 lemons)

a pinch of fine salt

90 g/6 tablespoons unsalted butter, cut into 6 pieces, at room temperature

MAKES 250 ML/ 1 CUP

THIS JELLY RECIPE IS THE PERFECT ACCOMPANIMENT TO PEANUT BUTTER AND TWO SLICES OF BREAD. PEELING GRAPES CAN BE A BIT OF A TEDIOUS PROCESS, BUT ONCE YOU TASTE THE JELLY, YOU'LL REALIZE IT WAS WORTH IT.

LEMON JUICE, ZEST AND A BIT OF SUGAR BRING OUT THE BEAUTIFUL PARTS OF WHAT LEMONS CAN REALLY TASTE LIKE. ANY VARIETAL CAN BE USED FROM REGULAR OLD LEMONS TO MEYER LEMONS FOR THIS SUBLIME RECIPE.

Grape Jelly

Preheat the oven to 75°C (150°F).

Peel the skins off the grapes. Set aside the grape skins; you will be using them later.

Put the pulp in a saucepan or pot and place over medium heat. Cover and cook for 5 minutes, stirring occasionally. When the grapes have broken down to a mush, remove them from the heat.

Place a large bowl in the sink and set a sieve/strainer over it. Pour the grape pulp into the sieve/strainer and, using a wooden spoon, push the pulp through the mesh. Discard the seeds.

Put the sugar in a baking pan and place in the low oven to warm.

Add the grape skin to the pulp and bring it to a boil, stirring occasionally. Boil for 2 minutes. The mixture will have turned dark thanks to the colour of the grape skins. Gradually add the warm sugar to the pulp, stirring in 250 ml/1 cup at a time. Bring back to a rolling boil and cook, stirring constantly. When it thickens, remove from the heat and let cool and solidify.

Lemon Curd

Fill a medium saucepan with 2.5–5 cm/ 1–2 inches of water and bring it to a simmer over high heat. Reduce the heat to low and keep the water at a bare simmer.

Place all of the ingredients except the butter in a large heatproof bowl and whisk to combine. Set the bowl over, but not touching, the simmering water and whisk constantly until the yolks thicken and the mixture forms ribbons when the whisk is lifted, about 7–10 minutes. (Check to ensure the water does not boil by periodically removing the bowl from the pan. If it boils, reduce the heat so the eggs do not curdle.)

Remove the bowl from the simmering water and whisk in the butter a piece at a time, waiting until each piece is completely melted and incorporated before adding another.

Set a fine-mesh sieve/strainer over a bowl. Strain the curd, pressing on the solids and scraping the curd on the underside of the mesh into the bowl. Discard the solids left in the strainer. Press clingfilm/plastic wrap directly onto the surface of the curd to prevent a skin from forming. Refrigerate until set and chilled, at least 3 hours.

Femme Fatale
& Brunch Punch

Femme fatale

450 g/8 oz. strawberries, hulled and quartered

2 tablespoons caster/granulated sugar or sugar syrup

1 tablespoon freshly squeezed lemon juice

pared zest of 1 lemon

250 ml/1 cup limoncello liqueur, well chilled

2 bottles brut Cava or Prosecco, well chilled

lemon twists or strawberry slices, to garnish

SERVES 10

Brunch punch

500 ml/2 cups gin

500 ml/2 cups Campari

500 ml/2 cups white vermouth

1.25 litres/5 cups grapefruit juice

500 ml/2 cups orange juice

cucumber and orange slices, to garnish

ice cubes, to serve

SERVES 10

DON'T BE FOOLED BY THIS DRINK'S LADYLIKE LOOKS – THE COMBINATION OF STRAWBERRIES, ITALIAN LIMONCELLO LIQUEUR AND SPARKLING WHITE WINE PACKS A PUNCH. IT'S SEDUCTIVE AND REFRESHING AND GREAT FOR SERVING TO A SUMMER CROWD.

Femme Fatale

Simply combine all the liquids in a punch bowl or large pitcher and stir gently.

Serve cold poured into Champagne flutes, or similar. Garnish with lemon twists or hulled and sliced strawberries just before serving.

THIS BRUNCH PUNCH IS SOPHISTICATED AS WELL AS DELICIOUS AND CAN BE SERVED BEFORE NOON OR LATE-NIGHT. THE WHITE VERMOUTH BALANCES OUT THE CAMPARI AND JUICES, MAKING IT A DRINK THAT EVERYONE (OF AGE!) WILL ENJOY.

Brunch Punch

Combine all the liquids in a punch bowl or large pitcher and stir gently. Float some of the cucumber and orange slices on the surface of the drink, reserving some to garnish the individual servings.

Ladle or pour the punch into rocks glasses filled with ice cubes, and garnish with extra fresh cucumber and orange slices just before serving.

COFFEE GRANITA & ESPRESSO MARTINIS

Coffee granita

270 g/9 tablespoons freshly ground espresso beans

about 5 tablespoons sugar

1.2 litres/5 cups boiling water

SERVES 4

Espresso martini

25 ml/1 oz. freshly made espresso

25 ml/2 oz. vodka

25 ml/2 oz. Tia Maria or other coffee-flavoured liqueur

orange zest curls, to garnish

SERVES 1

Almond espresso martini

25 ml/1 oz. freshly made espresso

35 ml/1¼ oz. vodka

20 ml/¾ oz. Amaretto, or other almond-flavoured liqueur

3 coffee beans and a pinch of toasted sliced/slivered almonds, to garnish

SERVES 1

A DELICIOUSLY REFRESHING AND NON-ALCOHOLIC TREAT, A SWEET COFFEE HIT MADE FOR SIPPING.

Coffee Granita

Brew fresh, strong coffee with the water and the ground espresso beans. Transfer the hot liquid to a cake pan or freezer-proof shallow bowl. Add sugar to taste, stirring to dissolve. Set aside to cool slightly, then transfer to the freezer and freeze, uncovered, for 1 hour.

Remove from the freezer, gently rake the tines of a fork across the surface of the coffee, breaking up any ice crystals in the middle and around the edges. Return to the freezer for a further 45 minutes, then repeat the process.

Repeat the freezing and raking process twice more until all of the coffee is frozen into flaky ice crystals. Spoon the granita into sundae bowls or martini glasses and serve with a teaspoon.

THE ESPRESSO MARTINI IS A MIX OF VODKA, FLAVOURED LIQUOR AND COFFEE WITH A KICK!

Espresso Martini

Pour all the ingredients into a shaker. Fill with ice and shake. Strain into a chilled martini glass. Wait for the cocktail to "separate" – a foam will rise to the top and the liquid below become clearer.

Garnish with the orange zest curls and serve immediately.

Almond Espresso Martini

Pour all the ingredients into a shaker. Fill with ice and shake. Strain into a chilled martini glass. Wait for the cocktail to "separate" – a foam will rise to the top and the liquid below become clearer.

Garnish with the coffee beans and flaked/slivered almonds. Serve immediately.

Blueberry Coffee & Italian Coffee

a pot of freshly brewed coffee (4 servings)

cream, to serve (optional)

blueberry coffee syrup (see recipe below)

Blueberry coffee syrup

250 g/2 cups fresh blueberries, washed

70 g/⅓ cup white sugar

SERVES 4

Italian coffee

600 ml/20 fl oz. freshly brewed coffee

4 teaspoons Amaretto, or other almond-flavoured liqueur

4 tablespoons Tia Maria, or other coffee-flavoured liqueur

about 175 ml/6 fl oz. whipping cream

sugar, to taste

SERVES 4

IT MIGHT SOUND LIKE AN UNLIKELY COMBINATION, BUT THE TWO FLAVOURS GO EXTREMELY WELL TOGETHER. THE RICH AND NEUTRAL FLAVOUR OF A BLUEBERRY MIXED WITH THE DARK FLAVOUR OF COFFEE HIGHLIGHT EACH OTHER WELL.

Blueberry Coffee

Put blueberries in a blender with 80 ml/⅓ cup water and blend until smooth. Strain to remove the seeds. Transfer the purée to a pan and add the sugar. Place over medium heat and stir constantly until the sugar is dissolved. Set the syrup aside to cool.

Brew the coffee to your liking. Add blueberry syrup and cream, if using, to taste. Serve immediately.

IN ITALY, AN "ITALIAN COFFEE" WOULD SIMPLY BE AN ESPRESSO. HOWEVER, IT'S ALSO A COCKTAIL PERFECT FOR THE BREAKFAST-FOR-DINNER CROWD. INSTEAD OF HAVING AN ORIGIN OF ITALY, IT'S JUST A PLAY ON THE POPULAR "IRISH" COFFEE.

Italian Coffee

Carefully pour 1 tablespoon of Tia Maria and 1 teaspoon of Amaretto into 4 heatproof glasses.

Top each glass up with hot coffee and stir. Taste and add sugar if needed (you may not need any at all).

Using the back of a teaspoon (or barspoon if you have one) gently pour the cream over the spoon and onto the surface of the drinks to "float" it on the top. Serve immediately.

THE PERFECT BLOODY MARY

seeds from 1 small cardamom pod (no more than 3–4 seeds)

¼–½ teaspoon black peppercorns

250 ml/1 cup high-quality passata (Italian strained tomatoes) or organic tomato juice

2 tablespoons Tamari soy sauce (or other soy sauce)

2 teaspoons Claret or other dry red wine

1 tablespoon agave nectar

freshly squeezed juice of 1 lemon

½ teaspoon paprika

½ teaspoon celery seeds

½ Habanero chilli/chile, deseeded and finely chopped

¼ teaspoon ground allspice

¼ teaspoon horseradish purée

½ teaspoon sea salt

To serve

ice cubes

100 ml/3½ oz. vodka

2 celery sticks, elegantly trimmed

MAKES 2

THIS COCKTAIL IS SPICY AND REFRESHING AT THE SAME TIME, WITH A LOVELY BALANCE OF SWEET, SAVOURY, SHARP AND SPICY NOTES. THIS IS THE PERFECT WELCOME DRINK FOR ANY SUMMER GET-TOGETHER; AND IF YOU HAVE DRAWN THE SHORT STRAW THE MIXER ITSELF MAKES A DELICIOUS ALCOHOL-FREE COCKTAIL.

Roughly grind together the cardamom seeds and peppercorns with a pestle and mortar. Put in a food processor with all the other ingredients and blend until smooth and fully combined. Pour into a bottle or jug/pitcher, cover and leave for several hours to allow the flavours to infuse and mingle.

To serve, put ice into two tall glasses. In each glass add half the vodka and half the tomato juice mixture. Mix with a trimmed stick of celery!

Tip: Take the half Habanero chilli/chile from the tip of the chilli/chile, as this is likely to be slightly less hot – you can always add more later, or even a dash of hot sauce.

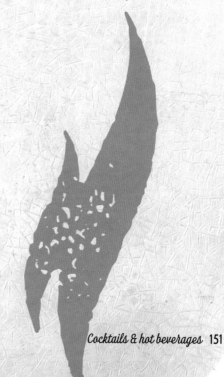

PICKLE-BACK MARTINI & THE SERGEANT PEPPER

Pickle-back martini

500 ml/2 cups gin or rye whiskey, as preferred

1 teaspoon dry vermouth (only if using gin)

4 tablespoons chilled dill pickle juice

4 dill pickle spears

a dash of hot sauce

ice

SERVES 4

The sergeant Pepper

150 ml/5 fl oz. gin

30 ml/1 fl oz. Black Pepper Simple Syrup (see below)

2 dessert apples, sliced into cubes

ice, for shaking and serving

Black pepper syrup

30 g/¼ cup crushed black peppercorns

200 g/1 cup sugar

SERVES 4

PICKLE JUICE IS NOT AN EASY-SELL WHEN IT COMES TO COCKTAILS. THIS DRINK, HOWEVER, IS THE PERFECT CURE FOR A HANGOVER. IT'S A PLAY ON A POPULAR DRINK CALLED THE PICKLE-BACK, WHICH IS A SHOT CHASED WITH PICKLE JUICE. IT'S A WONDERFUL DRINK, BUT NOT FOR THE FAINT HEARTED.

Pickle-back Martini

Make in two batches. Combine half the liquid ingredients in a shaker filled with ice. Shake for 30 seconds and strain into two chilled martini glasses. Repeat for the second batch and serve immediately.

THIS COCKTAIL IS ESSENTIALLY A CLASSIC MARTINI MIXED WITH HIGHLIGHTS OF BLACK PEPPER AND FRESH APPLE. IT'S WARM WITH FLORAL NOTES AND HAS A SPICY FINISH. NAMED AFTER THE FAMOUS BEATLES SONG – IT'S A DRINK THAT ANYONE (FAN OR NOT) SHOULD TRY AT LEAST ONCE.

The Sergeant Pepper

In a medium saucepan set over medium heat, combine the pepper and sugar with 250 ml/1 cup water. Stir until sugar dissolves, then remove from heat. Let cool (use an ice bath if needed immediately).

Make in two batches. Muddle half of the apple in a glass. Pour the gin and Black Pepper Simple Syrup into a shaker. Fill with ice and shake for 20–30 seconds. Strain into two glasses. Serve as a martini or on the rocks, as preferred.

Hot Chocolate
with cinnamon
& Cinnamon Coffee

Hot chocolate with cinnamon

30 g/1 oz. 100% dark/bittersweet chocolate, very finely chopped

500 ml/2 cups full-fat/whole milk

2 tablespoons caster/granulated sugar

½ teaspoon ground cinnamon, to serve

2 cinnamon sticks

SERVES 2

Cinnamon coffee

2 cinnamon sticks, broken into pieces

2½ tablespoons brown sugar

2 tablespoons freshly ground coffee beans

SERVES 4

THIS WARMING, COMFORTING DRINK IS A WINNER WHETHER YOU'RE STARTING OR ENDING YOUR DAY WITH IT. THIS IS A PROPER HOT CHOCOLATE – NO COCOA POWDER IN SIGHT.

Hot chocolate with cinnamon

Put all the ingredients in a medium saucepan over high heat. Heat, stirring constantly with a whisk, until the mixture comes to the boil.

Immediately remove from the heat and whisk vigorously for 1 minute.

Divide between two cups and pop a cinnamon stick in each one.

ADDING CINNAMON TO YOUR CUP OF COFFEE TRANSFORMS IT FROM A BREAKFAST PICK-ME-UP TO AN AFTER-DINNER LUXURY TO BE SAVOURED AND SIPPED.

Cinnamon coffee

Put 1 litre/4 cups water, the sugar and cinnamon into a large saucepan over high heat. Bring to the boil, then boil for 3 minutes.

Remove from the heat and add the coffee. Allow to infuse for 5 minutes.

Using a fine sieve/strainer, drain the coffee, then serve straight away while it is hot.

Oatmeal & Cinnamon Drink

120 g/1 cup oatmeal

750 ml/3 cups full-fat/whole milk

100 g/⅔ cup (dark) raisins

2 cinnamon sticks, broken into big pieces

5 tablespoons agave syrup

Serves 4–6

ATOLE DE AVENA IS A HOT, THICK, CINNAMON-FLAVOURED DRINK. THE "ATOLE" PART IS THE TRADITIONAL MEXICAN MILK-BASED DRINK THAT IS THICKENED WITH A GRAIN SUCH AS OATMEAL OR RICE. CHOCOLATE IS ANOTHER POPULAR VERSION (KNOWN AS "CHAMPURRADO") BUT THIS RECIPE USES CINNAMON. AGAVE SYRUP IS USED TO SWEETEN THE DRINK BECAUSE IT HAS A MORE NATURAL FLAVOUR THAN SUGAR. AGAVE SYRUP IS A NATURAL SWEETENER; IT HAS NONE OF THE BITTER AFTERTASTE ASSOCIATED WITH ARTIFICIAL SWEETENERS.

Put the oatmeal and 1 litre/4 cups water in a large saucepan over medium heat and bring to the boil.

Turn the heat down to low and cook for 2–3 minutes, stirring constantly, until the oatmeal has thickened and absorbed all the water.

Add the milk, raisins, cinnamon and agave syrup and bring to the boil, stirring constantly.

Reduce the heat to low and simmer very gently for 1 minute to allow it to thicken slightly.

Divide the drink between 4–6 cups, making sure that each cup gets some raisins.

INDEX

ACKNOWLEDGEMENTS

First and foremost, I would like to thank Cindy Richards and David Peters for being such wonderful publishers. It's truly, always a pleasure to work with the RPS team. Next, from the very bottom of my heart, I would like to thank all the authors and photographers whose work is included in this delicious compilation. Reading over the recipe list, I was floored at such creativity and it really set a bar for my own contributions. I am honoured to create recipes alongside such awesome cooks and chefs, whose work is brought to life by these amazing genius of photography. One of the things I have learned being a writer of cookbooks is that the author is really just a quarter of the book. As authors and cooks, it's our job to create the recipe – but then it is handed over to an editor, a designer, an art director, a food stylist and a prop stylist, who alongside the photographer, bring it all to life – with just one person getting most of the credit – the author. So that being said, I'd now like to give a big thank you to all of you. I would like to especially thank Julia Charles and Nathan Joyce who worked together to masterfully compile this new recipe collection and bring all of these talented people together in one great book. And last but not least, you – the reader. It's because of you that we all get to do what we do. Thank you.

RECIPE CREDITS

All recipes by Carol Hilker with the following exceptions:

DAN MAY

Baked chilli eggs

Cajun-spiced souffled baked potatoes

Devilled bubble and squeak

Habenero marmalade

Huevos rancheros

Nasi goreng

Spanish tortilla with roasted piquillo peppers

The perfect bloody mary

Trini saltfish buljol

UYEN LUU

Beef stew with star anise

Lemongrass beef baguette

Omelette baguette

LAURA WASHBURN

Mac 'n' cheese sandwich

Monte cristo

HELEN GRAVES

Mexican torta

The hot brown

HANNAH MILES

Welsh rarebit waffles

Ginger and sesame waffles with steak and dipping sauce

Potato waffles with barbecue beans

Huevos rancheros waffle

Buttermilk pancakes with salmon and horseradish cream

Beer and bacon pancakes

Courgette and feta griddle cakes

Squash and goats' cheese pancakes

Granola pancakes with salty honey sauce

Wake-me-up coffee Oreo pancakes

Peanut butter and jelly French toast

LOUISE PICKFORD

Shio ramen with pork and eggs

BEN FORDHAM & FELIPE FUENTES CRUZ

Fried corn tortillas (chilaquiles rojos)

Chayote and grapefruit salad

Hot chocolate with cinnamon

Cinnamon coffee

Oatmeal and cinnamon drink (atole de avena)

PICTURE CREDITS

PETER CASSIDY

19, 20, 23–27, 39, 40, 81, 92, 95, 98, 99, 115, 139, 150, 154, 157

STEVE PAINTER

43, 44, 52–56, 59, 103, 104, 111, 112, 116, 120, 123

TOBY SCOTT

1–17, 28–35, 48, 51, 60–78, 82–85, 88, 91, 97, 100–102, 107, 108, 119, 124–128, 131–136, 140–149, 153, 160

IAN WALLACE

87

ROB WHITE & STEPHEN CONROY

46, 47

CLARE WINFIELD

36, 37, 96